SPECTRUM®

Math

Grade 2

Published by Spectrum®
an imprint of Carson-Dellosa Publishing LLC
Greensboro, NC

Spectrum®
An imprint of Carson-Dellosa Publishing LLC
P.O. Box 35665
Greensboro, NC 27425 USA

ISBN 978-0-7696-3692-4

09-031127811

Table of Contents Grade 2

Table of Contents, continued

Chapter 9 Preparing for Algebra

NAME ______________________

Check What You Know

Counting and Writing through 99

Count from the right.

Circle the third duck. Underline the seventh duck.

Which duck is gray? The ________ duck.

Count tens and ones. Complete.

_____ tens _____ ones = ______

_____ ten _____ ones = ______

_____ tens _____ ones = ______

_____ tens _____ ones = ______

Write odd or even.

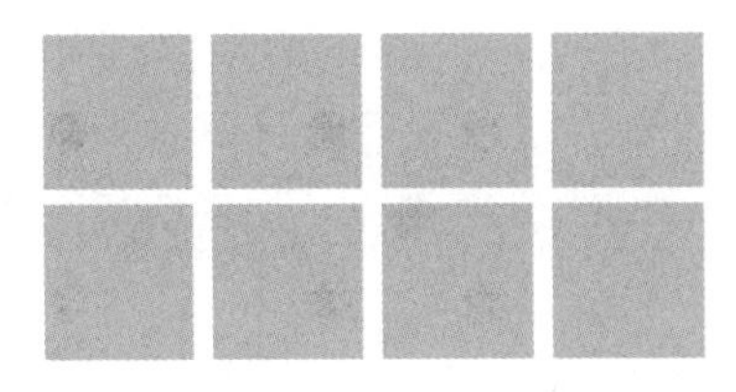

____

____

NAME ______________________

Check What You Know

Counting and Writing through 99

Count how many.

Write the number. _____ Write the number word. __________

Write the number. _____ Write the number word. __________

Count by 10.

10¢, _____¢, _____¢, 40¢, _____¢, _____¢

Complete the fact family.

$2 + \_\_\_ = 7$ $5 + 2 = \_\_\_$ $7 - \_\_\_ = 2$ $7 - \_\_\_ = 5$

Count by 5.

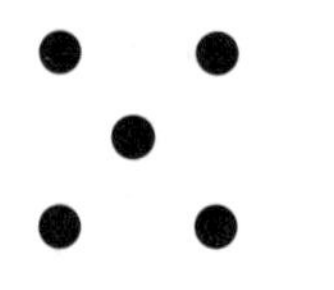 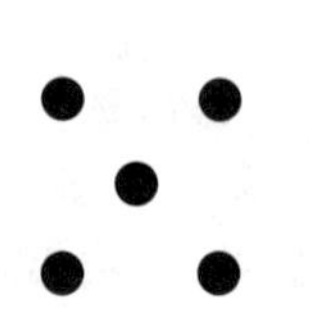 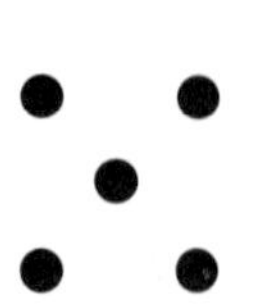 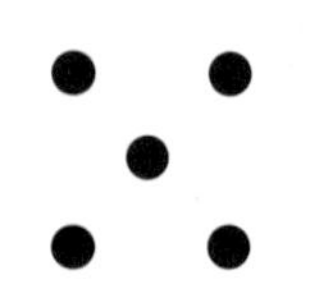 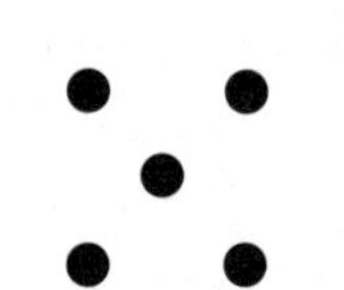 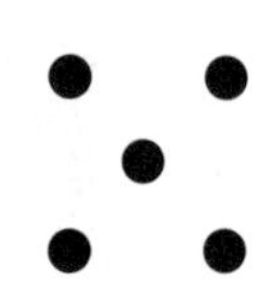

5, _____, 15, _____, _____, _____

NAME ______________________

Lesson 1.1 Counting and Writing 0 through 10

four	six	three	two

4	6	3	2

nine	eight	ten
	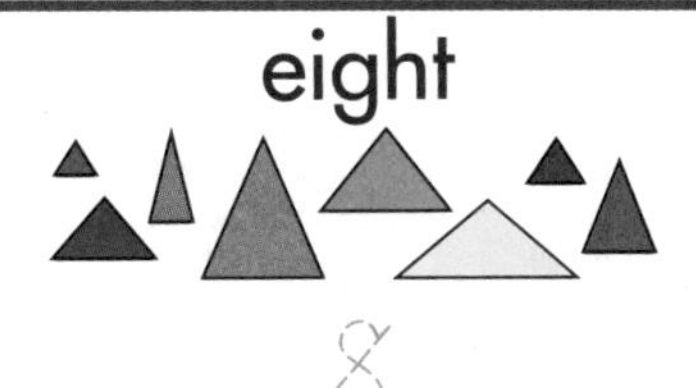	 
9	8	10

seven	zero	one	five

7	0	1	5

Write the number word.

 seven ______

 ______

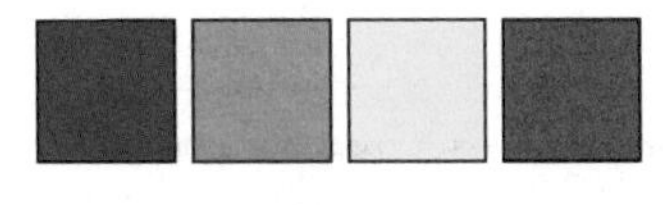  ______

 ______

 ______

 ______

 ______

 ______

 ______

NAME ____________________

Lesson 1.1 Counting and Writing 11 through 20

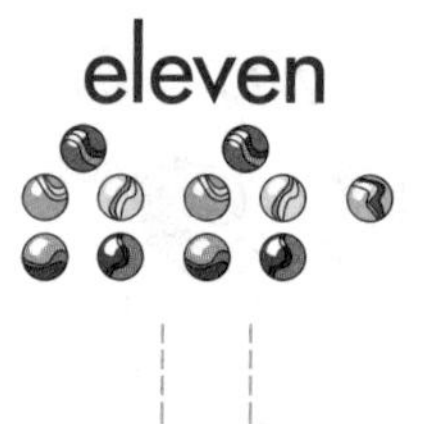

eleven	twelve	thirteen	fourteen	fifteen
11	12	13	14	15

sixteen	seventeen	eighteen	nineteen	twenty
16	17	18	19	20

Write the number or number word.

 eighteen

 ____________

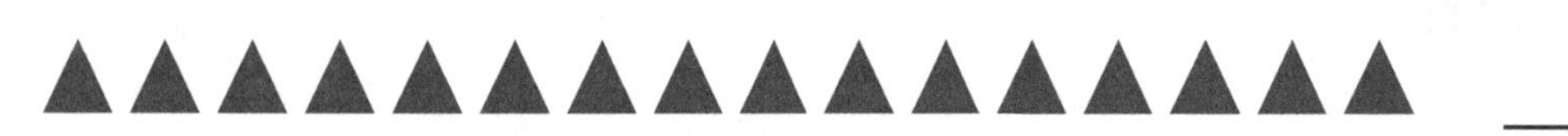 ____________

 ____________

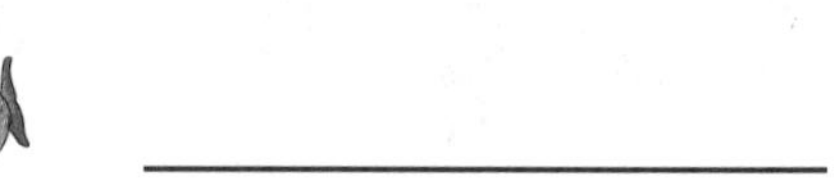

 19

 ____________

 ____________

 ____________

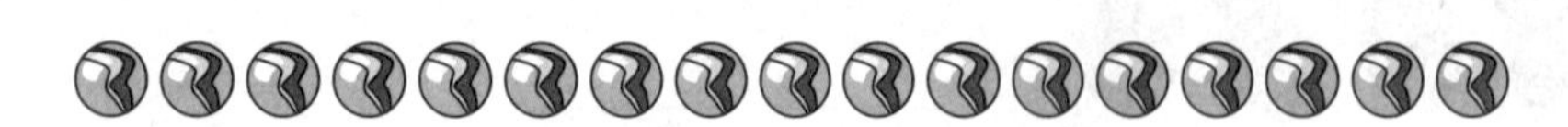 ____________

NAME ____________________

Lesson 1.2 Ordinal Position

Think about ordinal numbers.

Which puppy is black?

Count from the left. The __sixth__ puppy.

Count from the right. The __fifth__ puppy.

Count from the left.

Circle the third animal.

Underline the sixth animal.

Where in the line is the cow? ______

Where in the line are the two cats? ______, ______

Count from the right.

Which fish is white? The ______ fish.

Which fish is black? The ______ fish.

Circle the sixth fish.

Underline the second fish.

NAME ____________________

Lesson 1.2 Ordinal Position

Count from here.

Where are the teddy bears? eighth, seventeenth

Where are the dinosaurs? ________, ________,

____

Underline the seventh toy.

Circle the thirteenth toy.

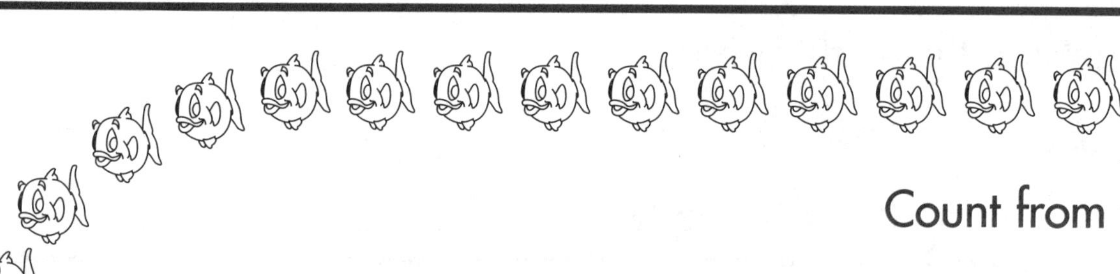

Count from here.

Color the third and tenth fish red.

Color the eighth and eighteenth fish blue.

Color the first, ninth, and fifteenth fish yellow.

NAME ___________________

Lesson 1.3 Counting Tens and Ones (1 through 10)

1¢

10¢

10¢

10 ones = 1 ten

Tell how many ones.

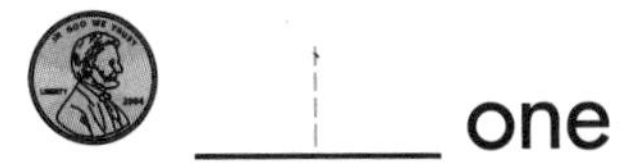 ______ one

 ______ ones

 ______ ones

 ______ ones

 ______ ones

 ______ ones

 ______ ones

 ______ ones

 ______ ones

 ______ ones

Tell how many tens and ones.

 0 ten 10 ones

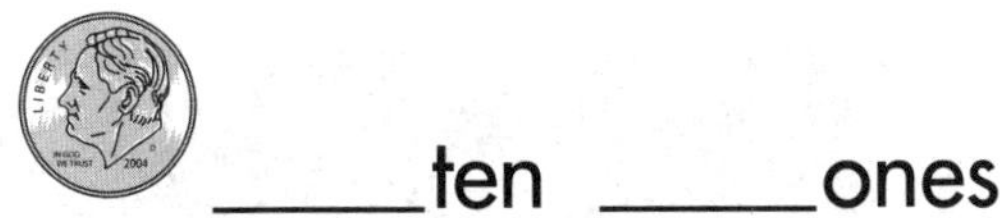 ______ ten ______ ones

NAME ______________________

Lesson 1.4 Counting Tens and Ones (11 through 19)

 = 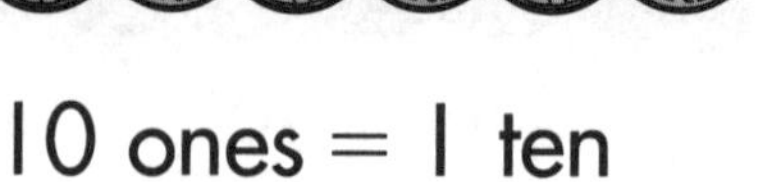

10 ones = 1 ten

1 ten 1 one = 11

Tell how many tens and ones.

__1__ ten __2__ ones = __12__

____ ten ____ ones = ______

____ ten ____ ones = ______

____ ten ____ ones = ______

____ ten ____ ones = ______

____ ten ____ ones = ______

____ ten ____ ones = ______

____ ten ____ ones = ______

NAME ____________________

Lesson 1.5 Counting Tens and Ones (20 through 29)

1 ten 10 ones = 2 tens = 20

Tell how many tens and ones.

2 tens 1 one = 21

_____ tens _____ ones = _______

_____ tens _____ ones = _______

_____ tens _____ ones = _______

_____ tens _____ ones = _______

_____ tens _____ ones = _______

_____ tens _____ ones = _______

_____ tens _____ ones = _______

_____ tens _____ ones = _______

NAME ____________________

Lesson 1.6 Counting Tens and Ones (30 through 49)

Tell how many tens and ones.

3 tens 0 ones = 30

3 tens 2 ones = 32

_____ tens _____ ones = _______

_____ tens _____ ones = _______

_____ tens _____ ones = _______

_____ tens _____ ones = _______

_____ tens _____ ones = _______

_____ tens _____ ones = _______

NAME ___________________________

Lesson 1.7 Counting Tens and Ones (50 through 99)

Tell how many tens and ones.

5 tens 0 ones = 50

5 tens 1 one = 51

_____ tens _____ ones = _______

_____ tens _____ ones = _______

_____ tens _____ ones = _______

_____ tens _____ ones = _______

_____ tens _____ ones = _______

_____ tens _____ ones = _______

NAME ____________________

Lesson 1.8 Skip Counting

Count by 2. Write the missing numbers.

2, 4, 6, __8__, 10, 12, ____

Count by 5. Write the missing numbers.

   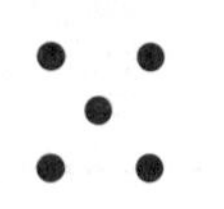 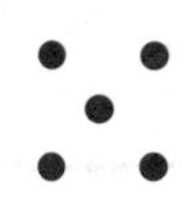 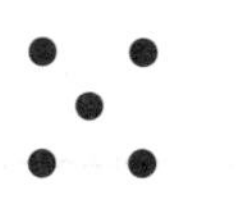 

5, 10, , ____, 25, ____, ____

Count by 10. Write the missing numbers.

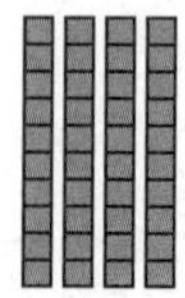 __40__ 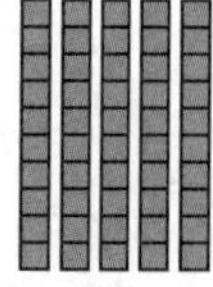 ____ 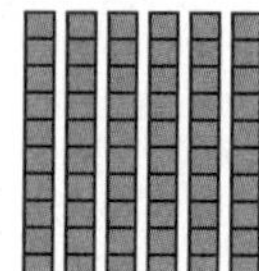 ____

Count by 2. Write the missing numbers.

12, __14__, ____, 18, 20, ____, 24, 26, 28

Count by 5. Write the missing numbers.

15, __20__, 25, ____, ____, 40, 45, 50

____, 60, ____, 70, ____, ____, 85

Count backward by 10. Write the missing numbers.

100, 90, __80__, 70, ____, 50, ____, ____, 20, 10

NAME ______________________________

Lesson 1.9 Money

A penny  is 1¢

A nickel  is 5¢ 

A dime  is 10¢ 

Count pennies by 2. Write the missing numbers.

2¢, 4¢, 6¢, __8__¢, ______¢, ______¢

Count by 2. Start at 80¢. Write the missing numbers.

80¢, 82¢, __84__¢, 86¢, ______¢, ______¢

Count by 5. Write the missing numbers.

5¢, __10__¢, 15¢, ______¢, 25¢, ______¢

NAME ______________________

Lesson 1.9 Money

Count by 5. Start at 50¢.

50¢, ___55___¢, 60¢, ______¢, 70¢, ______¢

Count by 10.

10¢, ___20___¢, 30¢, ______¢, ______¢, 60¢,

70¢, ______¢, ______¢, 100¢

Count backward by 10. Start at 100¢.

100¢, 90¢, ___80___¢, 70¢, ______¢, 50¢,

______¢, ______¢, ______¢, 10¢

NAME ______________________

Lesson 1.10 Odd or Even?

even

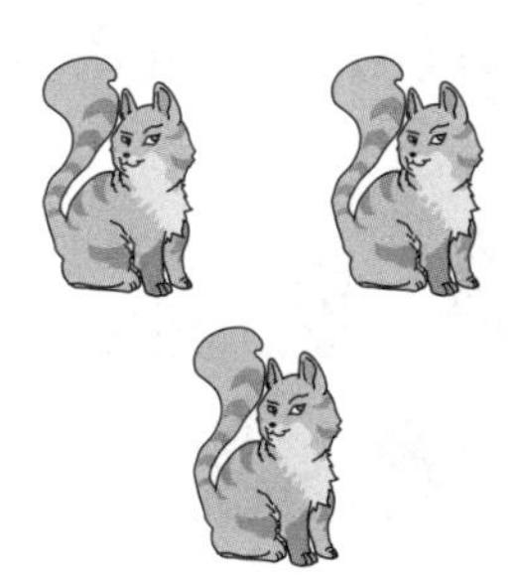

odd

odd

even

How many fish? 8

Odd or even? even

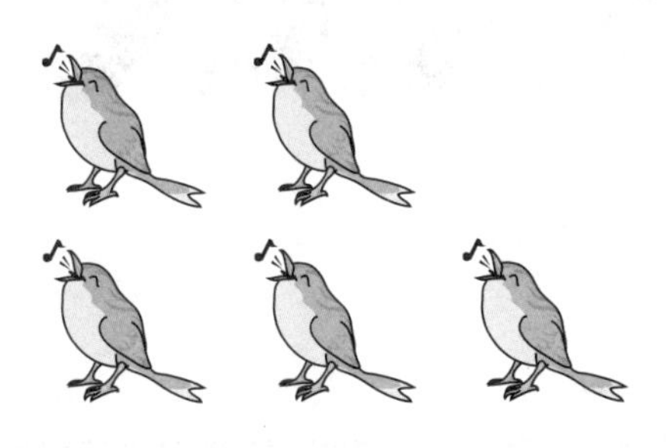

How many birds? ______

Odd or even? ______

NAME ________________________

Lesson 1.10 Odd or Even?

Circle the groups that are odd.

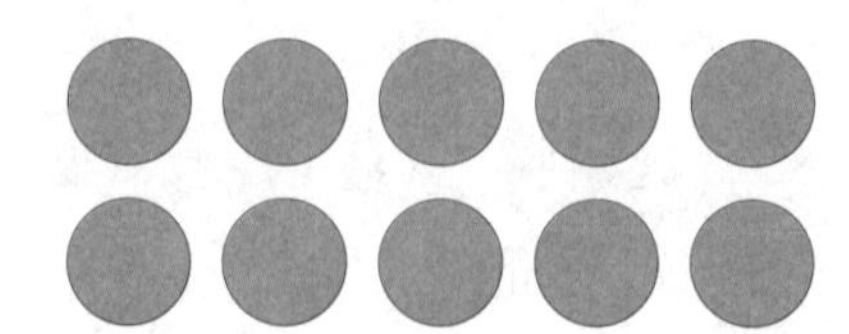

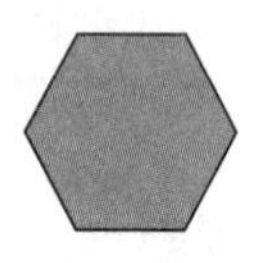

Tell how many. Label odd or even.

8 dolls

even

_____ cars

____

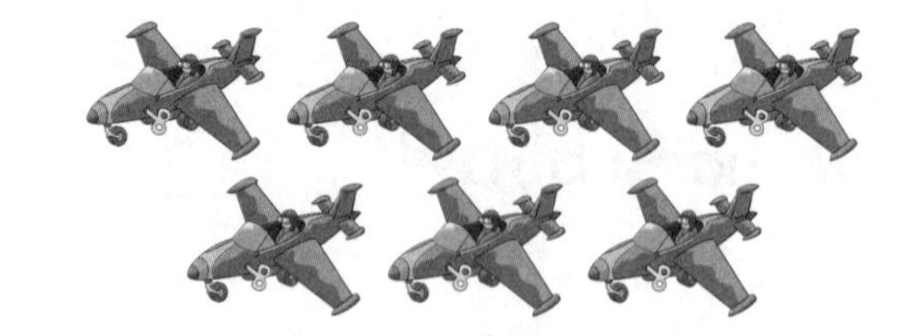

_____ jets

____

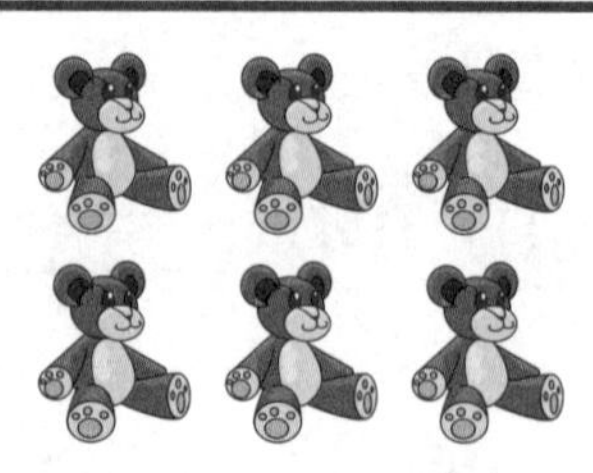

_____ bears

____

NAME ____________________

Lesson 1.11 Addition and Subtraction Facts

These facts are related.

$2 + 5 = 7$

$5 + 2 = 7$

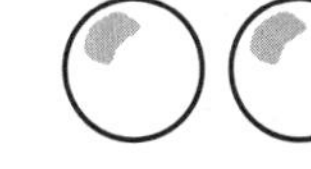   

$7 - 5 = 2$

$7 - 2 = 5$

Write the missing numbers.

$6 + 2 = 8$	$2 +$ _6_ $= 8$	$4 + 5 = 9$	$5 +$ ____ $= 9$
$8 -$ ____ $= 2$	$8 - 2 =$ ____	$9 -$ ____ $= 5$	$9 - 5 =$ ____
$3 + 2 = 5$	$2 + 3 =$ ____	$4 + 2 = 6$	$2 + 4 =$ ____
$5 -$ ____ $= 2$	$5 -$ ____ $= 3$	____ $- 4 = 2$	____ $- 2 = 4$

Complete the missing facts.

$3 + 1 = 4$, _1_ + _3_ = _4_, $4 - 1 = 3$, ____ − ____ = ____

$9 - 6 = 3$, ____ − ____ = ____, $3 + 6 = 9$, ____ + ____ = ____

$7 + 1 = 8$, ____ + ____ = ____, $8 - 1 = 7$, ____ − ____ = ____

NAME ____________________

Lesson 1.12 Grouping Objects

Group objects into threes.

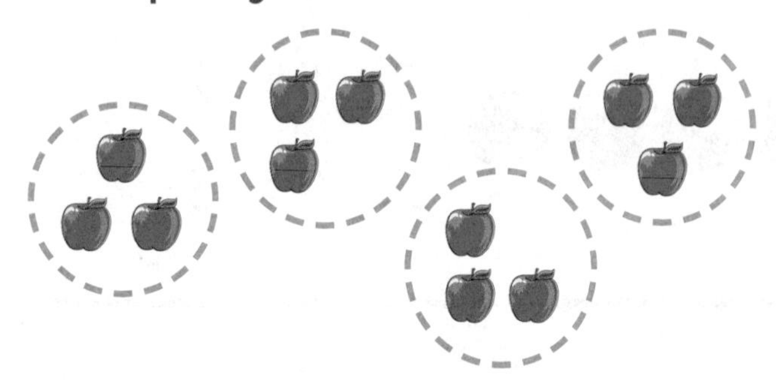

How many groups of 3? 4

How many are left? 0

Group objects into fours.

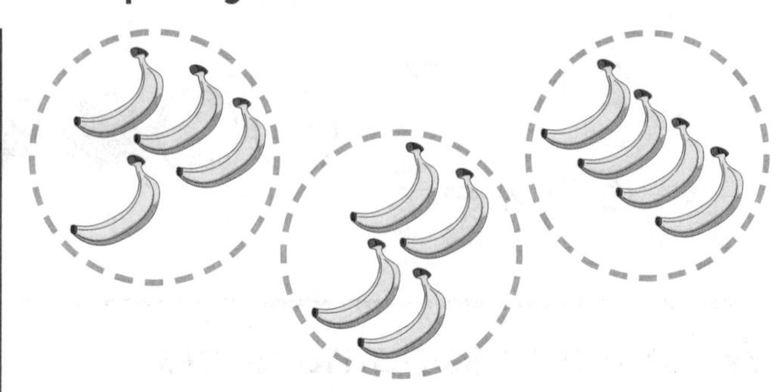

How many groups of 4? ______

How many are left? ______

Group objects into threes.

How many groups of 3? ______

How many are left? ______

How many groups of 3? ______

How many are left? ______

Group objects into fours.

How many groups of 4? ______

How many are left? ______

How many groups of 4? ______

How many are left? ______

NAME ______________________

Check What You Learned

Counting and Writing through 99

Count by 2. Start at 20.

   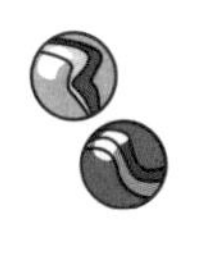  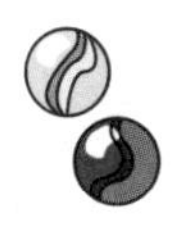

20, ______, ______, 26, ______, ______

Count by 5.

5¢, ______, ______, 20¢, ______, ______

Count how many.

Write the number. ______ Write the number word. __________

Write the number. ______ Write the number word. __________

Count tens and ones.

_____ tens _____ ones = ______

_____ tens _____ ones = ______

CHAPTER 1 POSTTEST

NAME ____________________

Check What You Learned

Counting and Writing through 99

Count tens and ones.

____ tens ____ ones = ______

____ tens ____ ones = ______

Write even or odd.

____

____

Group objects into threes.

How many groups of 3? ______

How many are left? ______

Complete the fact family.

$3 + \_\_\_ = 9$, $6 + 3 = \_\_\_$, $9 - \_\_\_ = 6$, $\_\_\_ - 6 = 3$

Count from the left.

Circle the twelfth fish. Underline the seventh fish.

NAME ____________________

Check What You Know

Addition and Subtraction Facts through 18

Add.

$7 + 9$	$2 + 3$	$0 + 2$	$3 + 8$	$5 + 2$	$7 + 8$
$4 + 4$	$9 + 1$	$8 + 4$	$3 + 1$	$2 + 7$	$9 + 8$
$2 + 1$	$6 + 0$	$7 + 6$	$5 + 9$	$9 + 3$	$6 + 4$

Subtract.

$5 - 4$	$14 - 7$	$6 - 4$	$10 - 5$	$13 - 5$	$18 - 9$
$11 - 4$	$7 - 0$	$9 - 6$	$4 - 4$	$16 - 8$	$15 - 9$
$17 - 8$	$8 - 5$	$3 - 0$	$10 - 3$	$12 - 4$	$7 - 2$

NAME ______________________

Check What You Know

SHOW YOUR WORK

Addition and Subtraction Facts through 18

Solve each problem.

Brian borrows 6 books from the library.

Jamal borrows 8 books.

How many books do they borrow in all? ________

There are 17 slices of pizza.

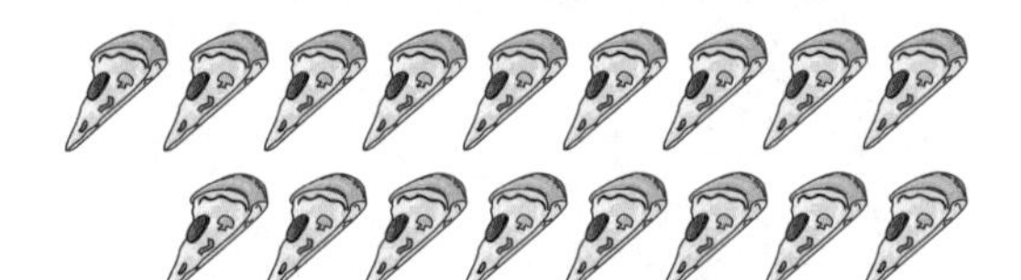

8 of them get eaten.

How many slices are left? ________

15 students are in the library.

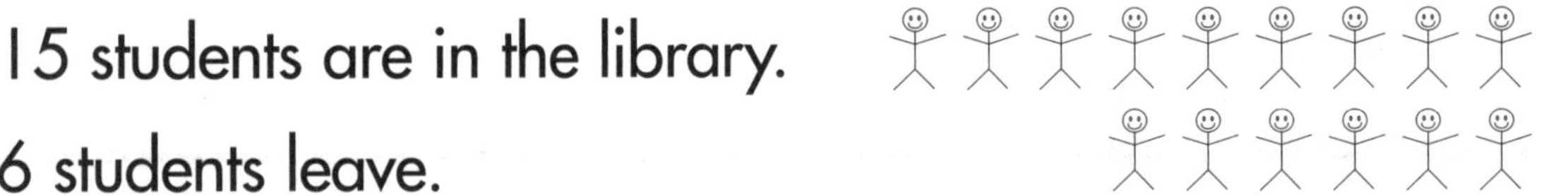

6 students leave.

How many students are still in the library? ________

Nina borrows 8 books.

Sue borrows 6 books.

How many more books does Nina borrow? ________

There are 8 desks on the first floor.

There are 7 desks on the second floor.

How many desks are there on the two floors? ________

Lesson 2.1 Adding through 5

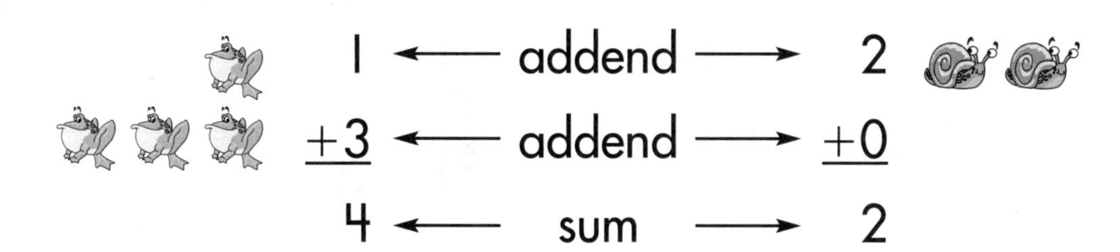

Add.

$\begin{array}{r} 2 \\ +3 \\ \hline 5 \end{array}$	$\begin{array}{r} 2 \\ +2 \\ \hline \end{array}$	$\begin{array}{r} 1 \\ +4 \\ \hline \end{array}$	$\begin{array}{r} 4 \\ +0 \\ \hline \end{array}$	$\begin{array}{r} 0 \\ +1 \\ \hline \end{array}$	$\begin{array}{r} 2 \\ +1 \\ \hline \end{array}$
$\begin{array}{r} 0 \\ +2 \\ \hline \end{array}$	$\begin{array}{r} 1 \\ +1 \\ \hline \end{array}$	$\begin{array}{r} 5 \\ +0 \\ \hline \end{array}$	$\begin{array}{r} 1 \\ +2 \\ \hline \end{array}$	$\begin{array}{r} 1 \\ +3 \\ \hline \end{array}$	$\begin{array}{r} 3 \\ +0 \\ \hline \end{array}$
$\begin{array}{r} 3 \\ +1 \\ \hline \end{array}$	$\begin{array}{r} 0 \\ +0 \\ \hline \end{array}$	$\begin{array}{r} 3 \\ +2 \\ \hline \end{array}$	$\begin{array}{r} 0 \\ +4 \\ \hline \end{array}$	$\begin{array}{r} 2 \\ +2 \\ \hline \end{array}$	$\begin{array}{r} 0 \\ +2 \\ \hline \end{array}$
$\begin{array}{r} 1 \\ +0 \\ \hline \end{array}$	$\begin{array}{r} 4 \\ +1 \\ \hline \end{array}$	$\begin{array}{r} 0 \\ +3 \\ \hline \end{array}$	$\begin{array}{r} 1 \\ +3 \\ \hline \end{array}$	$\begin{array}{r} 2 \\ +3 \\ \hline \end{array}$	$\begin{array}{r} 2 \\ +0 \\ \hline \end{array}$
$\begin{array}{r} 0 \\ +0 \\ \hline \end{array}$	$\begin{array}{r} 1 \\ +1 \\ \hline \end{array}$	$\begin{array}{r} 0 \\ +5 \\ \hline \end{array}$	$\begin{array}{r} 2 \\ +1 \\ \hline \end{array}$	$\begin{array}{r} 3 \\ +1 \\ \hline \end{array}$	$\begin{array}{r} 1 \\ +4 \\ \hline \end{array}$

NAME ____________________

Lesson 2.2 Subtracting from 0 through 5

There are 4 fish. 2 swim away.

How many fish are left?

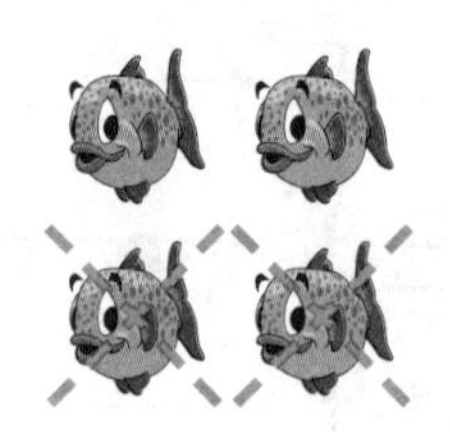

$$\begin{array}{r} 4 \\ -2 \\ \hline 2 \end{array} \leftarrow \text{difference}$$

Subtract.

$\begin{array}{r} 4 \\ -1 \\ \hline 3 \end{array}$	$\begin{array}{r} 3 \\ -3 \\ \hline \end{array}$	$\begin{array}{r} 1 \\ -1 \\ \hline \end{array}$	$\begin{array}{r} 5 \\ -4 \\ \hline \end{array}$	$\begin{array}{r} 3 \\ -0 \\ \hline \end{array}$	$\begin{array}{r} 5 \\ -2 \\ \hline \end{array}$
$\begin{array}{r} 2 \\ -2 \\ \hline \end{array}$	$\begin{array}{r} 1 \\ -0 \\ \hline \end{array}$	$\begin{array}{r} 5 \\ -5 \\ \hline \end{array}$	$\begin{array}{r} 4 \\ -3 \\ \hline \end{array}$	$\begin{array}{r} 5 \\ -3 \\ \hline \end{array}$	$\begin{array}{r} 4 \\ -0 \\ \hline \end{array}$
$\begin{array}{r} 5 \\ -1 \\ \hline \end{array}$	$\begin{array}{r} 4 \\ -2 \\ \hline \end{array}$	$\begin{array}{r} 2 \\ -0 \\ \hline \end{array}$	$\begin{array}{r} 0 \\ -0 \\ \hline \end{array}$	$\begin{array}{r} 3 \\ -1 \\ \hline \end{array}$	$\begin{array}{r} 4 \\ -1 \\ \hline \end{array}$
$\begin{array}{r} 2 \\ -1 \\ \hline \end{array}$	$\begin{array}{r} 5 \\ -0 \\ \hline \end{array}$	$\begin{array}{r} 4 \\ -4 \\ \hline \end{array}$	$\begin{array}{r} 5 \\ -2 \\ \hline \end{array}$	$\begin{array}{r} 2 \\ -2 \\ \hline \end{array}$	$\begin{array}{r} 3 \\ -3 \\ \hline \end{array}$
$\begin{array}{r} 3 \\ -2 \\ \hline \end{array}$	$\begin{array}{r} 4 \\ -1 \\ \hline \end{array}$	$\begin{array}{r} 5 \\ -4 \\ \hline \end{array}$	$\begin{array}{r} 4 \\ -2 \\ \hline \end{array}$	$\begin{array}{r} 3 \\ -0 \\ \hline \end{array}$	$\begin{array}{r} 5 \\ -1 \\ \hline \end{array}$

NAME ____________________

Lesson 2.3 Adding to 6, 7, and 8

5		1
+3		+6
8 ←	sum	→ 7

Add.

0 +6 6	4 +4	1 +6	3 +4	6 +2	8 +0
3 +3	5 +1	7 +0	2 +4	5 +3	7 +1
4 +3	2 +5	1 +7	6 +1	4 +2	6 +0
0 +8	5 +3	5 +2	2 +6	1 +5	0 +7
3 +5	4 +4	3 +4	2 +4	3 +3	1 +6

NAME ______________________

Lesson 2.4 Subtracting from 6, 7, and 8

There are 7 balls.

5 are baseballs.

How many are not baseballs?

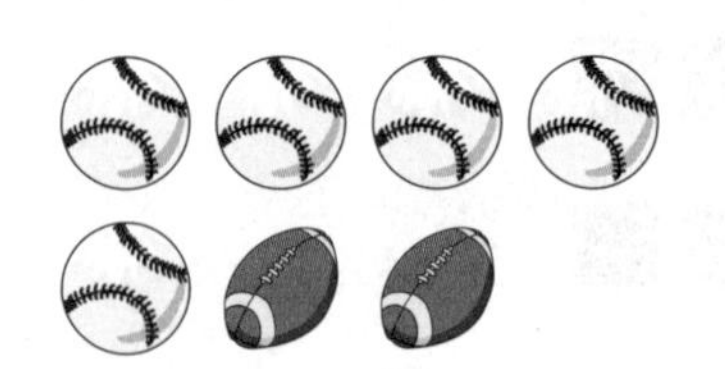

$$\begin{array}{r} 7 \\ -5 \\ \hline 2 \end{array}$$

Subtract.

$\begin{array}{r} 8 \\ -4 \\ \hline \end{array}$	$\begin{array}{r} 7 \\ -1 \\ \hline \end{array}$	$\begin{array}{r} 6 \\ -3 \\ \hline \end{array}$	$\begin{array}{r} 7 \\ -3 \\ \hline \end{array}$	$\begin{array}{r} 8 \\ -5 \\ \hline \end{array}$	$\begin{array}{r} 6 \\ -2 \\ \hline \end{array}$
$\begin{array}{r} 7 \\ -0 \\ \hline \end{array}$	$\begin{array}{r} 8 \\ -7 \\ \hline \end{array}$	$\begin{array}{r} 6 \\ -4 \\ \hline \end{array}$	$\begin{array}{r} 7 \\ -7 \\ \hline \end{array}$	$\begin{array}{r} 8 \\ -3 \\ \hline \end{array}$	$\begin{array}{r} 6 \\ -6 \\ \hline \end{array}$
$\begin{array}{r} 6 \\ -1 \\ \hline \end{array}$	$\begin{array}{r} 8 \\ -2 \\ \hline \end{array}$	$\begin{array}{r} 7 \\ -4 \\ \hline \end{array}$	$\begin{array}{r} 6 \\ -5 \\ \hline \end{array}$	$\begin{array}{r} 8 \\ -6 \\ \hline \end{array}$	$\begin{array}{r} 7 \\ -5 \\ \hline \end{array}$
$\begin{array}{r} 8 \\ -8 \\ \hline \end{array}$	$\begin{array}{r} 6 \\ -0 \\ \hline \end{array}$	$\begin{array}{r} 7 \\ -2 \\ \hline \end{array}$	$\begin{array}{r} 8 \\ -1 \\ \hline \end{array}$	$\begin{array}{r} 8 \\ -0 \\ \hline \end{array}$	$\begin{array}{r} 7 \\ -6 \\ \hline \end{array}$
$\begin{array}{r} 6 \\ -2 \\ \hline \end{array}$	$\begin{array}{r} 8 \\ -3 \\ \hline \end{array}$	$\begin{array}{r} 8 \\ -4 \\ \hline \end{array}$	$\begin{array}{r} 7 \\ -3 \\ \hline \end{array}$	$\begin{array}{r} 7 \\ -7 \\ \hline \end{array}$	$\begin{array}{r} 6 \\ -3 \\ \hline \end{array}$

NAME ______________________________

Lesson 2.5 Adding to 9 and 10

6	5
+3	+5
9 ← sum	→ 10

Add.

$8 + 1$	$2 + 8$	$4 + 6$	$3 + 6$	$7 + 3$	$5 + 4$
$7 + 2$	$9 + 0$	$8 + 2$	$5 + 5$	$9 + 1$	$0 + 9$
$6 + 3$	$1 + 8$	$3 + 6$	$4 + 5$	$2 + 7$	$6 + 4$
$5 + 4$	$1 + 9$	$7 + 3$	$3 + 7$	$0 + 9$	$8 + 1$
$7 + 2$	$5 + 5$	$9 + 1$	$6 + 4$	$2 + 8$	$4 + 5$

NAME ______________________

Lesson 2.6 Subtracting from 9 and 10

Dani has 10 postage stamps. 

	10
Felix has 6 postage stamps.	-6
How many more stamps does Dani have?	4 ← difference

Subtract.

9	10	9	10	10	9
-6	-5	-3	-4	-9	-7
10	9	9	10	9	10
-1	-8	-5	-8	-1	-6
9	9	10	9	10	10
-0	-4	-7	-2	-3	-0
9	10	9	10	10	9
-9	-2	-3	-9	-1	-5
9	10	9	9	10	10
-8	-5	-1	-7	-8	-3

NAME ______________________

Lesson 2.7 Adding to 11, 12, and 13

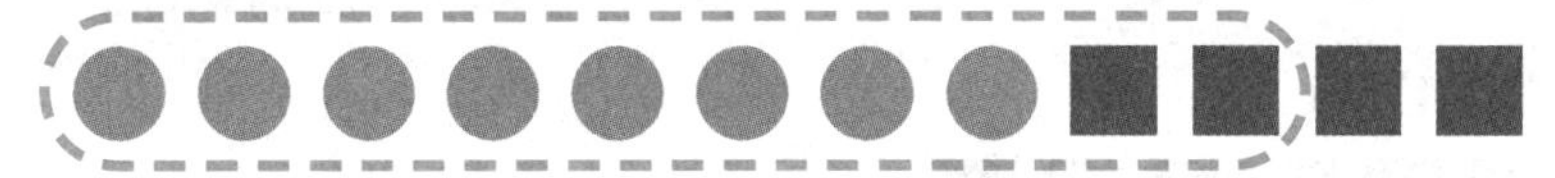

$8 + 4 = 10 + 2 = \underline{12}$

$6 + 7 = 10 + 3 = \underline{13}$

Add.

$3 + 9$	$4 + 7$	$7 + 6$	$9 + 2$	$4 + 8$	$6 + 5$
$6 + 6$	$9 + 4$	$5 + 7$	$9 + 3$	$7 + 4$	$5 + 8$
$5 + 6$	$8 + 4$	$3 + 8$	$6 + 7$	$2 + 9$	$4 + 9$
$8 + 5$	$8 + 3$	$7 + 5$	$9 + 3$	$7 + 6$	$6 + 5$
$9 + 2$	$5 + 7$	$6 + 6$	$5 + 8$	$9 + 4$	$3 + 8$

NAME ______________________

Lesson 2.8 Subtracting from 11, 12, and 13

13 = 1 ten 3 ones

Cross out to solve.

$$\begin{array}{r} 13 \\ -5 \\ \hline 8 \end{array}$$

12 = 1 ten 2 ones

Cross out to solve.

$$\begin{array}{r} 12 \\ -7 \\ \hline 5 \end{array}$$

Subtract.

12 − 4	11 − 9	13 − 9	12 − 5	13 − 4	11 − 6
11 − 8	13 − 6	13 − 8	12 − 3	11 − 5	12 − 6
13 − 4	11 − 7	12 − 9	12 − 4	13 − 7	11 − 3
12 − 5	13 − 5	12 − 8	11 − 5	11 − 4	13 − 9
11 − 2	13 − 6	11 − 8	12 − 3	12 − 7	11 − 6

NAME ______________________

Lesson 2.9 Adding to 14, 15, and 16

7				10
+8		=		+5
15				15

Add.

9 + 5	4 + 8	8 + 8	5 + 8	7 + 7	2 + 9
4 + 7	5 + 9	9 + 4	9 + 7	6 + 6	7 + 9
6 + 8	8 + 7	3 + 9	8 + 3	8 + 6	6 + 7
6 + 9	7 + 5	9 + 3	7 + 4	9 + 6	7 + 8
7 + 6	9 + 5	5 + 6	7 + 9	9 + 2	6 + 8

NAME ______________________

Lesson 2.10 Subtracting from 14, 15, and 16

$$\begin{array}{r} 16 \\ -9 \\ \hline 7 \end{array}$$

Think:
16 = 1 ten 6 ones

$$\begin{array}{r} 15 \\ -6 \\ \hline 9 \end{array}$$

Cross out to solve.
15 = 1 ten 5 ones

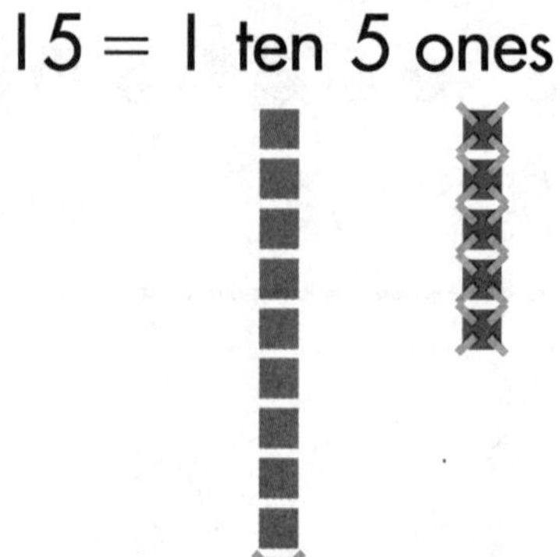

Subtract.

$\begin{array}{r} 14 \\ -\ 9 \\ \hline \end{array}$ $\begin{array}{r} 15 \\ -\ 8 \\ \hline \end{array}$ $\begin{array}{r} 13 \\ -\ 8 \\ \hline \end{array}$ $\begin{array}{r} 11 \\ -\ 3 \\ \hline \end{array}$ $\begin{array}{r} 14 \\ -\ 7 \\ \hline \end{array}$ $\begin{array}{r} 12 \\ -\ 8 \\ \hline \end{array}$

$\begin{array}{r} 11 \\ -\ 6 \\ \hline \end{array}$ $\begin{array}{r} 16 \\ -\ 7 \\ \hline \end{array}$ $\begin{array}{r} 14 \\ -\ 8 \\ \hline \end{array}$ $\begin{array}{r} 12 \\ -\ 5 \\ \hline \end{array}$ $\begin{array}{r} 13 \\ -\ 4 \\ \hline \end{array}$ $\begin{array}{r} 11 \\ -\ 5 \\ \hline \end{array}$

$\begin{array}{r} 14 \\ -\ 5 \\ \hline \end{array}$ $\begin{array}{r} 13 \\ -\ 6 \\ \hline \end{array}$ $\begin{array}{r} 15 \\ -\ 7 \\ \hline \end{array}$ $\begin{array}{r} 11 \\ -\ 9 \\ \hline \end{array}$ $\begin{array}{r} 12 \\ -\ 6 \\ \hline \end{array}$ $\begin{array}{r} 14 \\ -\ 6 \\ \hline \end{array}$

$\begin{array}{r} 13 \\ -\ 9 \\ \hline \end{array}$ $\begin{array}{r} 12 \\ -\ 9 \\ \hline \end{array}$ $\begin{array}{r} 15 \\ -\ 9 \\ \hline \end{array}$ $\begin{array}{r} 16 \\ -\ 8 \\ \hline \end{array}$ $\begin{array}{r} 11 \\ -\ 2 \\ \hline \end{array}$ $\begin{array}{r} 15 \\ -\ 6 \\ \hline \end{array}$

$\begin{array}{r} 11 \\ -\ 4 \\ \hline \end{array}$ $\begin{array}{r} 16 \\ -\ 9 \\ \hline \end{array}$ $\begin{array}{r} 12 \\ -\ 7 \\ \hline \end{array}$ $\begin{array}{r} 13 \\ -\ 5 \\ \hline \end{array}$ $\begin{array}{r} 14 \\ -\ 9 \\ \hline \end{array}$ $\begin{array}{r} 14 \\ -\ 7 \\ \hline \end{array}$

NAME ______________________

Lesson 2.11 Adding to 17 and 18

9	⚽⚽⚽⚽⚽⚽⚽⚽⚽		10
+8	⚽⚽⚽⚽⚽⚽⚽⚽	=	+7
17			17

Add.

$9 + 9$	$8 + 9$	$9 + 7$	$5 + 8$	$6 + 5$	$3 + 9$
$5 + 9$	$4 + 7$	$6 + 9$	$8 + 4$	$8 + 7$	$9 + 8$
$8 + 9$	$7 + 7$	$5 + 7$	$9 + 4$	$6 + 6$	$8 + 6$
$2 + 9$	$8 + 5$	$9 + 9$	$7 + 8$	$7 + 5$	$8 + 3$
$3 + 8$	$9 + 5$	$7 + 6$	$9 + 8$	$8 + 8$	$7 + 4$

NAME ____________________

Lesson 2.12 Subtracting from 17 and 18

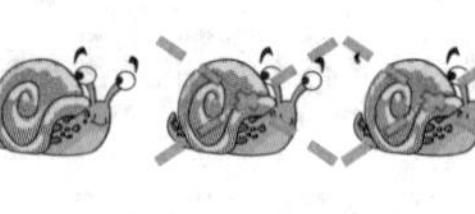

$$\begin{array}{r} 17 \\ -\ 9 \\ \hline 8 \end{array}$$

Subtract.

18 − 9	16 − 8	13 − 7	17 − 9	15 − 9	11 − 7
12 − 9	17 − 8	14 − 6	13 − 8	16 − 9	12 − 6
15 − 7	14 − 8	13 − 5	11 − 8	12 − 7	18 − 9
17 − 9	16 − 7	14 − 9	13 − 9	11 − 5	15 − 8
11 − 9	15 − 6	17 − 8	12 − 8	14 − 7	11 − 3

NAME ______________________

Lesson 2.13 Problem Solving

SHOW YOUR WORK

Solve each problem.

Steve has 7 fish.

Ramon has 13 fish.

How many more fish does Ramon have? 6

$$\begin{array}{r} 13 \\ -\ 7 \\ \hline 6 \end{array}$$

Yolanda has 8 teddy bears.

Maria has 6 teddy bears.

How many do they have in all? ______

Gina bakes 15 cupcakes.

Her friends eat 7.

How many cupcakes are left? ______

---

6 students are in the classroom.

Then, 3 more students go in.

How many students are in the classroom now? ______

Mark has 18 toy cars.

He gives 9 away.

How many cars does he have left? ______

NAME ______________________

Lesson 2.13 Problem Solving

SHOW YOUR WORK

Solve each problem.

Yoko picks 12 flowers.
She gives 6 to her mother.
How many flowers does Yoko have now?
Will you add or subtract? subtract Solve.

$$\begin{array}{r} 12 \\ -\ 6 \\ \hline 6 \end{array}$$

Taylor has 14 books.
5 of them are about sports.

How many of them are not about sports?
Will you add or subtract? __________ Solve.

Jesse mows 6 lawns.
Martin mows 7 lawns.

How many lawns do they mow in all?
Will you add or subtract? __________ Solve.

Kiki has 5 books. Sara has 4 books.
How many books do they have in all?

Will you add or subtract? __________ Solve.

NAME ______________________

Check What You Learned

Addition and Subtraction Facts through 18

Add.

$3 + 4$ | $8 + 2$ | $5 + 7$ | $2 + 1$ | $9 + 7$ | $9 + 9$

$1 + 8$ | $6 + 7$ | $5 + 1$ | $0 + 4$ | $9 + 5$ | $3 + 2$

$6 + 2$ | $4 + 5$ | $8 + 7$ | $9 + 8$ | $5 + 6$ | $3 + 9$

Subtract.

$13 - 4$ | $7 - 1$ | $4 - 2$ | $14 - 8$ | $10 - 9$ | $5 - 0$

$11 - 4$ | $15 - 6$ | $6 - 6$ | $17 - 8$ | $8 - 2$ | $12 - 6$

$16 - 8$ | $18 - 9$ | $9 - 5$ | $3 - 3$ | $11 - 8$ | $9 - 9$

NAME ____________________

Check What You Learned

SHOW YOUR WORK

Addition and Subtraction Facts through 18

Solve each problem.

There are 15 bananas.

Joe takes 6.

How many bananas are left? ________

The Changs have 7 apples. 

Mrs. Chang buys 5 more. 

How many apples do they have now? ________

The store has 12 boxes of plums. 

5 boxes of plums are sold.

How many boxes are left? ________

Grace buys 9 bananas. 

Her sister buys 9 more.

How many bananas do they buy in all? ________

Mrs. Lopez has 11 hats. 

3 of the hats have bows.

How many hats do not have bows? ________

NAME ______________________

Check What You Know

Adding and Subtracting 2-Digit Numbers (no renaming)

Add.

26 +31	34 +40	22 +76	53 + 6	16 +53
17 +42	81 +10	34 + 5	24 +34	42 +51
14 13 +12	46 20 + 2	16 41 +21	22 30 +44	40 16 + 3

Subtract.

46 −41	77 −50	63 −43	19 − 6	35 −13
57 −33	88 −61	97 −47	29 −12	48 −45
39 − 4	44 −13	67 −61	99 −79	54 −32

NAME ______________________

Check What You Know

SHOW YOUR WORK

Adding and Subtracting 2-Digit Numbers (no renaming)

Solve each problem.

Patrick sees 24 .

Mara sees 41 .

How many  do they see? ________

---

36 are on the lake.

22 are on the shore.

How many are there in all? ________

The store has 37 .

It has 25 . How many more

does it have than  ________?

---

58 are on the field.

45 of the are playing soccer.

How many are not playing soccer? ________

Martina spends 53¢    .

Dave spends 41¢ .

How much more does Martina spend? ________¢

NAME ______________________

Lesson 3.1 Adding 2-Digit Numbers

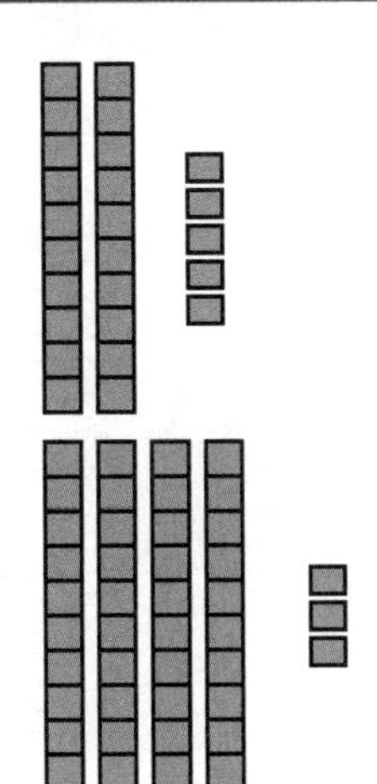

First add ones. Then, add tens.

25	25	25
+43	+43	+43
	8	sum = 68

Add to find the sum.

53 +11 = 64	36 +43	74 + 5	26 +61	40 +34
25 +51	44 + 4	15 +72	82 +12	66 +22
31 +60	57 +32	91 + 7	46 +23	52 +37
17 +70	28 +41	82 + 3	65 +14	35 +24
84 +11	27 +50	18 +80	38 +21	33 +20

NAME ____________________

Lesson 3.1 Adding 2-Digit Numbers

Add.

63 + 6 (69)	42 + 55 (97)	29 + 10	71 + 8	62 + 13
45 + 54	19 + 60	30 + 9	16 + 41	22 + 64
30 + 26	81 + 7	47 + 2	56 + 11	48 + 20
15 + 34	67 + 1	42 + 21	56 + 20	39 + 50
23 + 33	17 + 52	44 + 12	16 + 32	86 + 13
90 + 4	31 + 45	68 + 10	24 + 34	36 + 41
73 + 5	25 + 64	75 + 3	58 + 40	51 + 12

NAME ______________________

Lesson 3.2 Addition Practice

Add.

53 +14 67	83 + 6 89	65 +20	18 +61	12 +27
62 + 7	71 +13	66 +11	16 +31	27 +60
46 +43	55 + 2	19 +70	74 +22	16 +53
73 +12	14 +13	44 +50	35 +54	10 +30
91 + 5	72 + 5	26 +41	33 +51	40 +25
24 +45	81 +13	34 +52	56 +11	37 +50
30 +19	36 + 3	12 +42	83 + 4	67 +10

NAME ___________________

Lesson 3.2 Problem Solving

SHOW YOUR WORK

Solve each problem.

Marti catches 10 in one pond.
She catches 11 in another pond.
How many does she catch in all? 21

$$\begin{array}{r} 10 \\ +\ 11 \\ \hline 21 \end{array}$$

There are 42 in one tree.
There are 33 in another tree.
How many are in both trees? ______

Craig finds 13 .
Zach finds 20 .
How many do they find in all? ______

There were 14 in the park in the morning.
There were 22 in the park at night.
How many were in the park in all? ______

There are 32 in one flock.
There are 27 in another flock.
How many are there in all? ______

NAME ____________________

Lesson 3.3 Subtracting 2-Digit Numbers

$$\begin{array}{r} 77 \\ -26 \\ \hline \end{array}$$

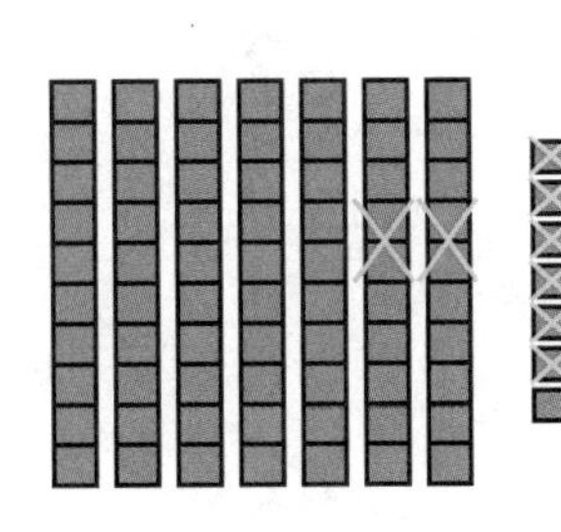

First, subtract the ones.

$$\begin{array}{r} 77 \\ -26 \\ \hline 1 \end{array}$$

Then, subtract the tens.

$$\begin{array}{r} 77 \\ -26 \\ \hline 51 \end{array}$$

Subtract.

$\begin{array}{r} 49 \\ -39 \\ \hline 10 \end{array}$	$\begin{array}{r} 87 \\ -\ \ 6 \\ \hline 81 \end{array}$	$\begin{array}{r} 36 \\ -24 \\ \hline \end{array}$	$\begin{array}{r} 54 \\ -40 \\ \hline \end{array}$	$\begin{array}{r} 68 \\ -16 \\ \hline \end{array}$
$\begin{array}{r} 79 \\ -63 \\ \hline \end{array}$	$\begin{array}{r} 78 \\ -25 \\ \hline \end{array}$	$\begin{array}{r} 42 \\ -12 \\ \hline \end{array}$	$\begin{array}{r} 19 \\ -\ \ 7 \\ \hline \end{array}$	$\begin{array}{r} 26 \\ -11 \\ \hline \end{array}$
$\begin{array}{r} 59 \\ -38 \\ \hline \end{array}$	$\begin{array}{r} 28 \\ -14 \\ \hline \end{array}$	$\begin{array}{r} 95 \\ -62 \\ \hline \end{array}$	$\begin{array}{r} 74 \\ -50 \\ \hline \end{array}$	$\begin{array}{r} 67 \\ -41 \\ \hline \end{array}$
$\begin{array}{r} 92 \\ -81 \\ \hline \end{array}$	$\begin{array}{r} 35 \\ -\ \ 5 \\ \hline \end{array}$	$\begin{array}{r} 77 \\ -17 \\ \hline \end{array}$	$\begin{array}{r} 82 \\ -51 \\ \hline \end{array}$	$\begin{array}{r} 86 \\ -64 \\ \hline \end{array}$
$\begin{array}{r} 58 \\ -53 \\ \hline \end{array}$	$\begin{array}{r} 75 \\ -61 \\ \hline \end{array}$	$\begin{array}{r} 47 \\ -37 \\ \hline \end{array}$	$\begin{array}{r} 89 \\ -27 \\ \hline \end{array}$	$\begin{array}{r} 65 \\ -60 \\ \hline \end{array}$

NAME ____________________

Lesson 3.3 Subtracting 2-Digit Numbers

Subtract.

91 − 80 = 11	46 − 23 = 23	57 − 32	83 − 33	69 − 55
34 − 21	48 − 22	73 − 52	56 − 23	76 − 45
65 − 13	44 − 20	96 − 85	66 − 31	90 − 70
43 − 10	72 − 30	88 − 71	94 − 84	29 − 5
99 − 8	18 − 4	26 − 22	86 − 55	39 − 27
78 − 64	93 − 3	59 − 25	82 − 50	77 − 36
97 − 72	69 − 8	74 − 12	16 − 3	46 − 35

NAME ____________________

Lesson 3.4 Subtraction Practice

Subtract.

$\begin{array}{r} 67 \\ -45 \\ \hline 22 \end{array}$	$\begin{array}{r} 54 \\ -20 \\ \hline 34 \end{array}$	$\begin{array}{r} 73 \\ -63 \\ \hline \end{array}$	$\begin{array}{r} 99 \\ -83 \\ \hline \end{array}$	$\begin{array}{r} 68 \\ -62 \\ \hline \end{array}$
$\begin{array}{r} 79 \\ -7 \\ \hline \end{array}$	$\begin{array}{r} 88 \\ -70 \\ \hline \end{array}$	$\begin{array}{r} 37 \\ -34 \\ \hline \end{array}$	$\begin{array}{r} 66 \\ -6 \\ \hline \end{array}$	$\begin{array}{r} 89 \\ -44 \\ \hline \end{array}$
$\begin{array}{r} 57 \\ -32 \\ \hline \end{array}$	$\begin{array}{r} 95 \\ -63 \\ \hline \end{array}$	$\begin{array}{r} 47 \\ -4 \\ \hline \end{array}$	$\begin{array}{r} 87 \\ -42 \\ \hline \end{array}$	$\begin{array}{r} 49 \\ -48 \\ \hline \end{array}$
$\begin{array}{r} 65 \\ -30 \\ \hline \end{array}$	$\begin{array}{r} 76 \\ -33 \\ \hline \end{array}$	$\begin{array}{r} 85 \\ -31 \\ \hline \end{array}$	$\begin{array}{r} 92 \\ -52 \\ \hline \end{array}$	$\begin{array}{r} 38 \\ -17 \\ \hline \end{array}$
$\begin{array}{r} 96 \\ -81 \\ \hline \end{array}$	$\begin{array}{r} 43 \\ -11 \\ \hline \end{array}$	$\begin{array}{r} 58 \\ -7 \\ \hline \end{array}$	$\begin{array}{r} 93 \\ -53 \\ \hline \end{array}$	$\begin{array}{r} 84 \\ -71 \\ \hline \end{array}$
$\begin{array}{r} 94 \\ -14 \\ \hline \end{array}$	$\begin{array}{r} 63 \\ -3 \\ \hline \end{array}$	$\begin{array}{r} 29 \\ -15 \\ \hline \end{array}$	$\begin{array}{r} 97 \\ -23 \\ \hline \end{array}$	$\begin{array}{r} 61 \\ -40 \\ \hline \end{array}$
$\begin{array}{r} 49 \\ -6 \\ \hline \end{array}$	$\begin{array}{r} 24 \\ -4 \\ \hline \end{array}$	$\begin{array}{r} 77 \\ -51 \\ \hline \end{array}$	$\begin{array}{r} 98 \\ -80 \\ \hline \end{array}$	$\begin{array}{r} 45 \\ -23 \\ \hline \end{array}$

Lesson 3.4 Problem Solving

SHOW YOUR WORK

Solve each problem.

Ms. Willis has 28 books.
Mr. Sanchez borrows 10 books.
How many books does Ms. Willis have left? 18

$$\begin{array}{r} 28 \\ -\ 10 \\ \hline 18 \end{array}$$

The first-grade class has 32 desks.
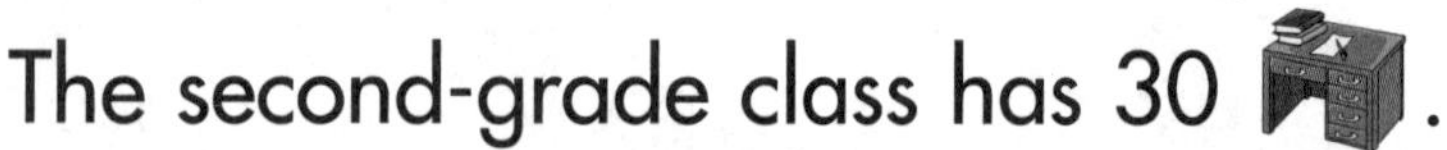
The second-grade class has 30 desks.
How many more  does the first-grade class have? ______

The art room has 65 pens.
Students are using 22 pens.
How many  are not being used? ______

Students had 44 milks at breakfast.
They had 59 milks at lunch. How many
more milks did students have at lunch? ______

The library has 37 books about computers.
12 of the books are being borrowed. How
many  about computers are still in the library? ______

Lesson 3.5 Adding Three Numbers

		Add the ones.	Add the tens.
23		23	23
44		44	44
+12		+12	+12
		9	79

Add.

13	62	44	16	22
50	11	23	40	32
+ 6	+15	+20	+12	+42
69				

22	30	71	12	33
44	10	12	20	20
+21	+ 9	+ 4	+33	+ 6

36	12	25	11	32
20	40	32	16	12
+13	+ 4	+ 1	+20	+22

25	10	44	30	21
11	24	11	24	37
+43	+ 5	+22	+14	+30

NAME ______________________

Lesson 3.5 Problem Solving

SHOW YOUR WORK

Solve each problem.

Lanie has 10  .
Tina has 12  . Paul has 25  .
How many  do they have in all? 47

$$\begin{array}{r} 10 \\ 12 \\ +\ 25 \\ \hline 47 \end{array}$$

The toy store sold 14  in March,
15  in April, and 20  in May.
How many  did the toy store sell in all? ______

Felicia puts 6  , 22  , and
30  on shelves. How many toys
does Felicia put on shelves? ______

The toy store has 32  , 26  ,
and 10  . How many of these toys
does the toy store have in all? ______

The bakery sells 14  on Monday, 23 
on Tuesday, and 30  on Wednesday.
How many  did the bakery sell? ______

NAME ____________________

Lesson 3.6 Problem Solving

Circle the most expensive item.

A pencil costs	A pen costs	A marker costs	A crayon costs

30¢	32¢	42¢	24¢

A pencil costs 30¢	A pen costs ___¢
A marker costs + 42¢	A crayon costs + ___¢
The two items cost 72¢	The two items cost ___¢

A pencil costs ___¢	A marker costs ___¢
A pen costs + ___¢	A crayon costs + ___¢
The two items cost ___¢	The two items cost ___¢

A pencil costs ___¢	A pen costs ___¢
A marker costs ___¢	A crayon costs ___¢
A crayon costs + ___¢	A pencil costs + ___¢
The three items cost ___¢	The three items cost ___¢

NAME ______________________

Lesson 3.6 Problem Solving

A banana costs	An apple costs	An orange costs	A melon costs

35¢	20¢	33¢	85¢

Which fruit costs the most? ____________

Which fruit costs the least? ____________

A melon costs 85¢ An orange costs − 33¢ A melon costs this much more. 52¢	An orange costs ¢ An apple costs − ¢ An orange costs this much more. ¢
A banana costs ¢ An apple costs − ¢ A banana costs this much more. ¢	A melon costs ¢ An apple costs − ¢ A melon costs this much more. ¢
A melon costs ¢ A banana costs − ¢ A melon costs this much more. ¢	A banana costs ¢ An orange costs − ¢ A banana costs this much more. ¢

NAME ____________________

Check What You Learned

Adding and Subtracting 2-Digit Numbers (no renaming)

Add.

42 +37	12 +24	90 + 3	22 +44	15 +42	63 +36
14 +33	22 + 6	14 +45	23 +35	72 +12	15 +20
11 23 +25	36 20 +12	14 10 + 3	12 52 +23	35 10 + 4	20 30 +19

Subtract.

79 −63	44 −20	68 −55	52 −11	85 −35	26 − 4
99 −46	76 − 6	19 −16	45 −12	76 −42	39 −15
77 − 4	64 −54	95 −70	37 − 7	29 −12	96 −52

CHAPTER 3 POSTTEST

NAME ___________________________

Check What You Learned

SHOW YOUR WORK

Adding and Subtracting 2-Digit Numbers (no renaming)

CHAPTER 3 POSTTEST

Solve each problem.

Kerry has 15 .

Janice has 14 .

How many  do they have in all? __________

Jermaine has 27 .

Brian has 31 .

How many do they have in all? __________

The class plants 35 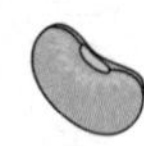 seeds.

The seeds grow into 24 plants.

How many 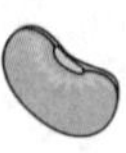 do not grow into plants? __________

Sydney makes 45 .

Rosa makes 65 .

How many more  does Rosa make? __________

Josh spends 45¢  at the bake sale.

Nate spends 52¢   at the bake sale.

How much do they spend in all? __________¢

NAME ________________

Check What You Know

Adding and Subtracting 2-Digit Numbers (with renaming)

Add.

45 +37	66 + 9	44 +19	65 +25	36 +47
17 +56	33 + 8	29 +28	57 +15	76 +19
64 +27	55 + 6	38 +46	12 +48	18 +26

Subtract.

93 −65	54 −49	23 − 5	63 −57	80 −42
33 −16	52 −24	85 −37	40 −18	77 −19
32 − 8	66 −59	70 −21	83 − 9	94 −67

NAME ____________________

Check What You Know

SHOW YOUR WORK

Adding and Subtracting 2-Digit Numbers (with renaming)

Solve each problem.

Anita picks 45 .

She picks 61 . How many

more  than  does she pick? ________

José picks 38 . He picks 35 .

How many pieces of fruit does José pick in all? ________

Max's bucket holds 72 .

Trey's bucket holds 44 .

How many more  does Max's bucket hold? ________

Paula picks 45 .

Carol picks 46 .

How many  do they pick in all? ________

The farm stand has 95  for sale.

The farm stand sells 38 .

How many  are left? ________

NAME ______________________

Lesson 4.1 Adding 2-Digit Numbers

Add the ones.	Put the ones in the ones place. Put the tens in the tens place.	Add the tens.
37 7 +45 +5 ? 12 12 = 1 ten 2 ones	1 37 +45 2	1 37 +45 sum = 82
46 6 +29 +9 ? 15 15 = 1 ten 5 ones	1 46 +29 5	1 46 +29 sum = 75

Add.

15 +66 81	48 +44	29 +35	19 +18	43 +39
75 +17	88 + 8	47 +37	26 +55	27 + 9
65 + 7	34 +28	46 + 5	69 +23	36 +49
54 +16	14 +59	45 +25	24 + 6	33 +58

NAME ______________________

Lesson 4.1 Adding 2-Digit Numbers

Add the ones.	Put the one in the ones place. Put the ten in the tens place.	Add the tens.
68 + 13 = ? 8 + 3 = 11 11 = 1 ten 1 one	1 (regrouped) 68 + 13 1	1 (regrouped) 68 + 13 sum = 81

Add.

12 + 78 = 90	56 + 7	67 + 3	11 + 79	26 + 38
32 + 18	74 + 9	45 + 15	53 + 19	29 + 13
57 + 14	52 + 39	16 + 64	77 + 8	48 + 12
28 + 27	63 + 17	35 + 6	25 + 59	47 + 23
65 + 5	44 + 38	24 + 37	11 + 49	46 + 36
27 + 46	53 + 18	19 + 45	29 + 18	32 + 49

NAME ____________________

Lesson 4.2 Addition Practice

Add the ones.	Put the one in the ones place. Put the ten in the tens place.	Add the tens.
$\begin{array}{r} 36 \\ +44 \\ \hline ? \end{array}$ $\begin{array}{r} 6 \\ +4 \\ \hline 10 \end{array}$ 10 = 1 ten 0 ones	$\begin{array}{r} 1 \\ 36 \\ +44 \\ \hline 0 \end{array}$	$\begin{array}{r} 1 \\ 36 \\ +44 \\ \hline \text{sum} = 80 \end{array}$

Add.

$\begin{array}{r} 13 \\ +58 \\ \hline 71 \end{array}$ $\begin{array}{r} 42 \\ +\ 9 \\ \hline \end{array}$ $\begin{array}{r} 26 \\ +57 \\ \hline \end{array}$ $\begin{array}{r} 38 \\ +22 \\ \hline \end{array}$ $\begin{array}{r} 15 \\ +49 \\ \hline \end{array}$

$\begin{array}{r} 55 \\ +18 \\ \hline \end{array}$ $\begin{array}{r} 32 \\ +29 \\ \hline \end{array}$ $\begin{array}{r} 56 \\ +\ 4 \\ \hline \end{array}$ $\begin{array}{r} 68 \\ +\ 7 \\ \hline \end{array}$ $\begin{array}{r} 39 \\ +28 \\ \hline \end{array}$

$\begin{array}{r} 33 \\ +\ 8 \\ \hline \end{array}$ $\begin{array}{r} 53 \\ +29 \\ \hline \end{array}$ $\begin{array}{r} 67 \\ +25 \\ \hline \end{array}$ $\begin{array}{r} 16 \\ +36 \\ \hline \end{array}$ $\begin{array}{r} 78 \\ +14 \\ \hline \end{array}$

$\begin{array}{r} 34 \\ +19 \\ \hline \end{array}$ $\begin{array}{r} 48 \\ +\ 3 \\ \hline \end{array}$ $\begin{array}{r} 24 \\ +47 \\ \hline \end{array}$ $\begin{array}{r} 35 \\ +\ 5 \\ \hline \end{array}$ $\begin{array}{r} 54 \\ +27 \\ \hline \end{array}$

$\begin{array}{r} 43 \\ +17 \\ \hline \end{array}$ $\begin{array}{r} 76 \\ +\ 6 \\ \hline \end{array}$ $\begin{array}{r} 23 \\ +69 \\ \hline \end{array}$ $\begin{array}{r} 46 \\ +19 \\ \hline \end{array}$ $\begin{array}{r} 59 \\ +13 \\ \hline \end{array}$

$\begin{array}{r} 72 \\ +18 \\ \hline \end{array}$ $\begin{array}{r} 27 \\ +56 \\ \hline \end{array}$ $\begin{array}{r} 34 \\ +29 \\ \hline \end{array}$ $\begin{array}{r} 19 \\ +65 \\ \hline \end{array}$ $\begin{array}{r} 36 \\ +49 \\ \hline \end{array}$

NAME ____________________

Lesson 4.2 Problem Solving

SHOW YOUR WORK

Solve each problem.

Cara has 35 .

Ben has 39 .

How many do they have in all? 74

$$\begin{array}{r} 35 \\ +\ 39 \\ \hline 74 \end{array}$$

Marcus has 48 .

May has 36 .

How many  do they have in all? ______

Pedro picks 33 .

Jessica picks 28 .

How many  do they pick in all? ______

There are 15 students with .

There are 9 students with .

How many students have  or ? ______

Toya picks 15 .

Jon picks 16 .

How many  do they pick in all? ______

NAME ______________________

Lesson 4.3 Subtracting 2-Digit Numbers

	Rename 1 ten as 10 ones.	Subtract the ones.	Subtract the tens.
33 − 19; 3 tens 3 ones = 2 tens 13 ones	2 13 ~~3~~~~3~~ −19	2 13 ~~3~~~~3~~ −19 4	2 13 ~~3~~~~3~~ −19 difference = 14
60 − 28; 6 tens 0 ones = 5 tens 10 ones	5 10 ~~6~~~~0~~ −28	5 10 ~~6~~~~0~~ −28 2	5 10 ~~6~~~~0~~ −28 difference = 32

Subtract.

36 − 7 29	51 −39	44 −15	84 −47	72 −65
76 −19	90 −78	53 −26	94 −85	75 −18
44 −29	83 −46	64 −59	50 −29	97 −78
66 −28	32 −17	40 −25	57 −29	61 − 5

NAME ____________________

Lesson 4.3 Subtracting 2-Digit Numbers

	Rename 1 ten as 10 ones.	Subtract the ones.	Subtract the tens.
41 −35	3 11 ~~41~~ −35	3 11 ~~41~~ −35 6	3 11 ~~41~~ −35 difference = 6 Should you write a number in the tens place? _____

Subtract.

72 −69 3	28 −19	66 −48	96 − 8	82 −37
80 −67	24 − 8	60 −43	54 −45	91 −55
42 −38	82 −56	92 −63	77 −68	81 −33
74 −58	86 −48	73 −49	95 −87	30 −14
46 −27	31 −23	71 −34	22 − 6	96 −69

NAME ______________________

Lesson 4.4 Subtraction Practice

	Rename 1 ten as 10 ones.	Subtract the ones.	Subtract the tens.
51 −23	4 11 ~~5~~ ~~1~~ −23	4 11 ~~5~~ ~~1~~ −23 8	4 11 ~~5~~ ~~1~~ −23 difference = 28

Subtract.

98 −89	20 − 3	11 − 2	46 −29	64 −38
71 −35	60 −15	22 −13	56 −28	44 −17
10 − 6	53 −25	74 −26	51 − 4	75 −39
42 −27	75 −46	82 −36	51 −25	97 −49
50 −14	82 −45	55 −47	72 −48	90 −41
76 −58	31 − 7	43 −34	62 −27	92 −36

NAME ______________________

Lesson 4.4 Problem Solving

SHOW YOUR WORK

Solve each problem.

Freddie finds 33 snails.

Tina finds 28 snails.

How many more snails does Freddie find? 5

$$\begin{array}{r} \overset{2\,13}{\cancel{3}\cancel{3}} \\ -\,2\,8 \\ \hline 5 \end{array}$$

Adam picks up 25 shells.

19 of the shells are broken.

How many of the shells are not broken? ______

Becky has 31 peanuts.

She eats 8 peanuts.

How many peanuts does she have left? ______

William has 26 cars.

He gives 8 of the cars to a friend.

How many cars does William have left? ______

Connie counts 42 fish.

Annie counts 27 fish.

How many more fish does Connie count? ______

NAME ___________________________

Check What You Learned

Adding and Subtracting 2-Digit Numbers (with renaming)

Add.

$\begin{array}{r}42\\+18\\\hline\end{array}$ $\begin{array}{r}79\\+\ 5\\\hline\end{array}$ $\begin{array}{r}85\\+\ 7\\\hline\end{array}$ $\begin{array}{r}44\\+29\\\hline\end{array}$ $\begin{array}{r}15\\+27\\\hline\end{array}$

$\begin{array}{r}35\\+28\\\hline\end{array}$ $\begin{array}{r}25\\+55\\\hline\end{array}$ $\begin{array}{r}34\\+19\\\hline\end{array}$ $\begin{array}{r}63\\+\ 9\\\hline\end{array}$ $\begin{array}{r}24\\+39\\\hline\end{array}$

$\begin{array}{r}47\\+\ 6\\\hline\end{array}$ $\begin{array}{r}12\\+38\\\hline\end{array}$ $\begin{array}{r}57\\+26\\\hline\end{array}$ $\begin{array}{r}49\\+11\\\hline\end{array}$ $\begin{array}{r}16\\+\ 8\\\hline\end{array}$

Subtract.

$\begin{array}{r}83\\-44\\\hline\end{array}$ $\begin{array}{r}68\\-59\\\hline\end{array}$ $\begin{array}{r}73\\-38\\\hline\end{array}$ $\begin{array}{r}30\\-24\\\hline\end{array}$ $\begin{array}{r}65\\-39\\\hline\end{array}$

$\begin{array}{r}53\\-35\\\hline\end{array}$ $\begin{array}{r}15\\-\ 9\\\hline\end{array}$ $\begin{array}{r}47\\-18\\\hline\end{array}$ $\begin{array}{r}75\\-37\\\hline\end{array}$ $\begin{array}{r}26\\-18\\\hline\end{array}$

$\begin{array}{r}84\\-46\\\hline\end{array}$ $\begin{array}{r}60\\-34\\\hline\end{array}$ $\begin{array}{r}76\\-29\\\hline\end{array}$ $\begin{array}{r}52\\-43\\\hline\end{array}$ $\begin{array}{r}42\\-27\\\hline\end{array}$

NAME ______________________________

Check What You Learned

SHOW YOUR WORK

Adding and Subtracting 2-Digit Numbers (with renaming)

Solve each problem.

Yumi picks 50 .

Kris picks 38 .

How many more  does Yumi pick? ________

The farm stand has two kinds of .

It has 57 of one kind and 39 of the other kind.

How many  does the farm stand have in all? ________

Ayisha buys 60 , and

51 of them are ripe.

How many of the  are not ripe? ________

Nick picks 42 . He sells 18 of

the  at the farm stand. How many

 does Nick have left? ________

The farm stand sells 37  on Saturday

and 29  on Sunday. How many

 does it sell in all? ________

NAME ______________________

Mid-Test Chapters 1–4

Add.

$\begin{array}{r} 4 \\ +9 \\ \hline \end{array}$ $\begin{array}{r} 28 \\ +15 \\ \hline \end{array}$ $\begin{array}{r} 44 \\ +\ 5 \\ \hline \end{array}$ $\begin{array}{r} 8 \\ +6 \\ \hline \end{array}$ $\begin{array}{r} 55 \\ +39 \\ \hline \end{array}$ $\begin{array}{r} 1 \\ +8 \\ \hline \end{array}$

$\begin{array}{r} 8 \\ +9 \\ \hline \end{array}$ $\begin{array}{r} 63 \\ +15 \\ \hline \end{array}$ $\begin{array}{r} 73 \\ +\ 8 \\ \hline \end{array}$ $\begin{array}{r} 0 \\ +5 \\ \hline \end{array}$ $\begin{array}{r} 23 \\ +46 \\ \hline \end{array}$ $\begin{array}{r} 2 \\ +6 \\ \hline \end{array}$

$\begin{array}{r} 12 \\ 23 \\ +\ 4 \\ \hline \end{array}$ $\begin{array}{r} 30 \\ 17 \\ +31 \\ \hline \end{array}$ $\begin{array}{r} 1 \\ +3 \\ \hline \end{array}$ $\begin{array}{r} 4 \\ +8 \\ \hline \end{array}$ $\begin{array}{r} 18 \\ +34 \\ \hline \end{array}$ $\begin{array}{r} 48 \\ +20 \\ \hline \end{array}$

Subtract.

$\begin{array}{r} 79 \\ -43 \\ \hline \end{array}$ $\begin{array}{r} 7 \\ -2 \\ \hline \end{array}$ $\begin{array}{r} 18 \\ -\ 9 \\ \hline \end{array}$ $\begin{array}{r} 43 \\ -15 \\ \hline \end{array}$ $\begin{array}{r} 12 \\ -\ 3 \\ \hline \end{array}$ $\begin{array}{r} 68 \\ -15 \\ \hline \end{array}$

$\begin{array}{r} 30 \\ -19 \\ \hline \end{array}$ $\begin{array}{r} 15 \\ -\ 8 \\ \hline \end{array}$ $\begin{array}{r} 10 \\ -\ 3 \\ \hline \end{array}$ $\begin{array}{r} 46 \\ -36 \\ \hline \end{array}$ $\begin{array}{r} 3 \\ -0 \\ \hline \end{array}$ $\begin{array}{r} 43 \\ -\ 6 \\ \hline \end{array}$

$\begin{array}{r} 14 \\ -\ 6 \\ \hline \end{array}$ $\begin{array}{r} 8 \\ -8 \\ \hline \end{array}$ $\begin{array}{r} 56 \\ -44 \\ \hline \end{array}$ $\begin{array}{r} 72 \\ -35 \\ \hline \end{array}$ $\begin{array}{r} 17 \\ -\ 9 \\ \hline \end{array}$ $\begin{array}{r} 9 \\ -4 \\ \hline \end{array}$

NAME ____________________

Mid-Test Chapters 1–4

Write the number. ________

Write the number word.

____

Is it odd or even? ________

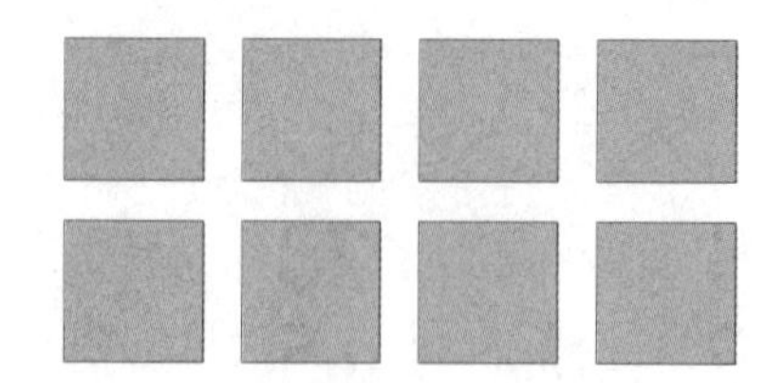

Write the number. ________

Write the number word.

____

Is it odd or even? ________

Count by 5. Start at 40.

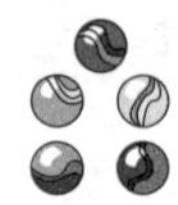   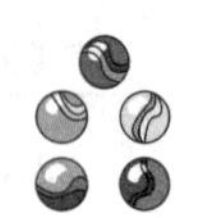 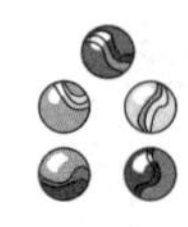 

40, 45, _____, _____, 60, _____

Count by 2. Start at 12¢.

12¢, _____¢, _____¢, 18¢, _____¢, _____¢

Count tens and ones.

_____ tens _____ ones = ______

_____ ten _____ ones = ______

_____ tens _____ ones = ______

_____ tens _____ ones = ______

CHAPTERS 1–4 MID-TEST

NAME ______________________

Mid-Test Chapters 1–4

Start counting from the arrow.

Circle the seventh frog.

Underline the fifteenth frog.

The gray frog is __________.

Complete the fact family.

$4 + 3 = \_\_\_$, $3 + \_\_\_ = 7$, $7 - \_\_\_ = 4$, $\_\_\_ - 4 = 3$

Group by 3.

How many groups of fish? ______

How many fish are left? ______

SHOW YOUR WORK

Solve each problem.

Pascal picks 14 .

Kim picks 13 .

How many do they pick in all? ______

The Williams family has 34 stuffed animals.

9 of them are .

How many of them are not ? ______

CHAPTERS 1–4 MID-TEST

NAME ____________________

Mid-Test Chapters 1–4

SHOW YOUR WORK

Solve each problem.

Emil has 12 . He lends
3 to Jeff. How many
 does Emil have left? ________

Terrence has 24 .
Bella has 22 . Mike has 21 .
How many  do they have in all? ________

An apple costs .
An orange costs .
How much do they cost? ________¢

The earth club plants 14  on Saturday
and 18 on Sunday.
How many  do they plant in all? ________

The earth club plants 45.
24 of the  are tulips.
How many of the  are not tulips? ________

CHAPTERS 1–4 MID-TEST

NAME ____________________

Check What You Know

Counting and Writing 3-Digit Numbers

Write the number shown.

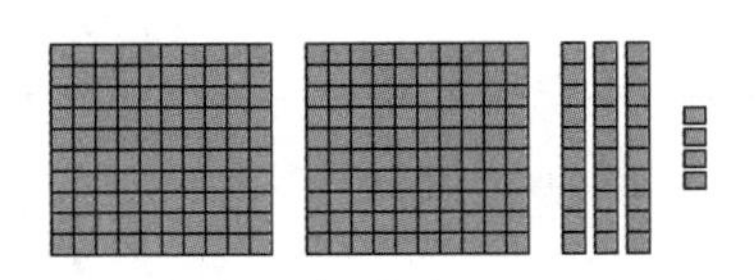

______

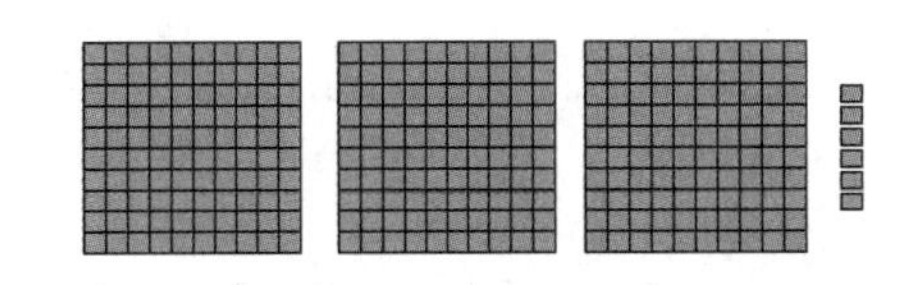

______

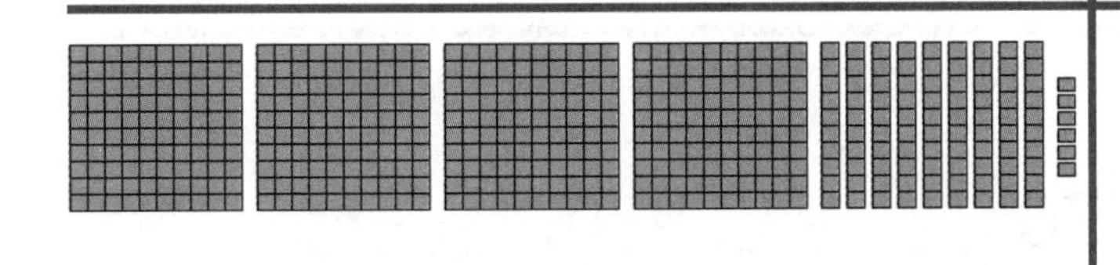

______

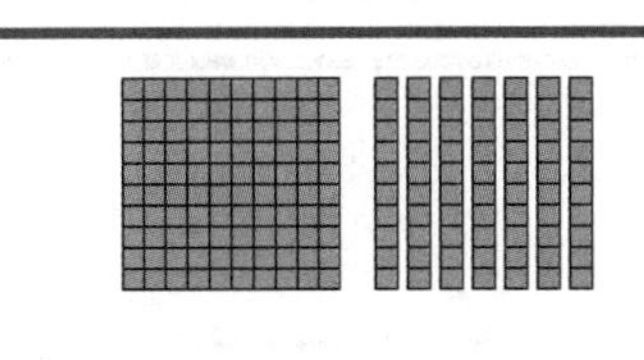

______

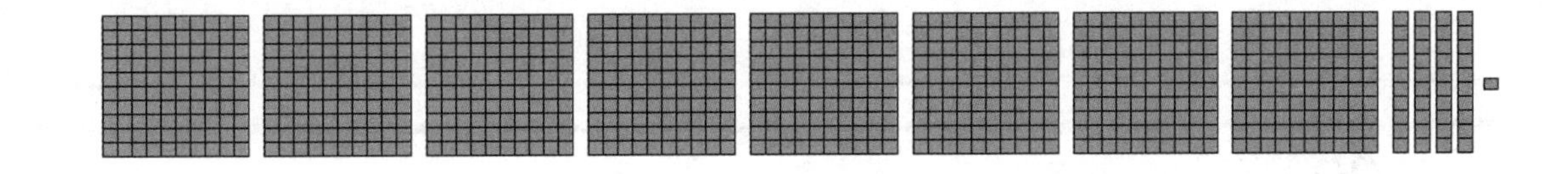

______

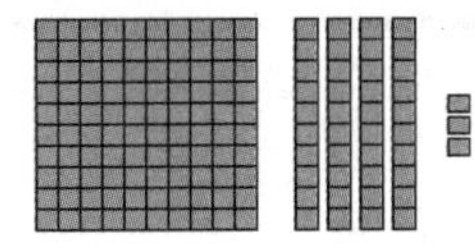

______

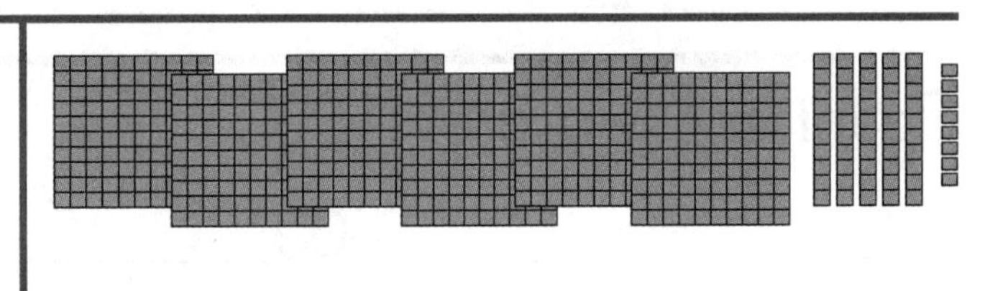

______

Round each number to the nearest 10.

75 ______	43 ______	32 ______	55 ______
46 ______	51 ______	37 ______	81 ______
14 ______	93 ______	24 ______	64 ______
89 ______	72 ______	68 ______	17 ______

NAME ________________

Check What You Know

Counting and Writing 3-Digit Numbers

Count by 10.

360, ______, ______, 390, 400, ______, ______, 430

720, 730, ______, ______, 760, ______, ______, 790

______, ______, 190, ______, ______, 220, ______, ______

Count by 5.

450, ______, ______, 465, 470, ______, 480, ______

890, ______, 900, ______, ______, 915, ______, ______

______, ______, 675, ______, ______, ______, ______, 700

Count by 100.

______, 200, ______, ______, 500, ______, ______

Count backward by 100.

______, ______, 600, ______, ______, 300, ______, ______

Compare numbers. Use >, <, or =.

460	☐	540	918	☐	908	103	☐	120
575	☐	590	260	☐	240	347	☐	298
701	☐	707	647	☐	742	818	☐	818
157	☐	120	450	☐	370	963	☐	993

NAME ______________________

Lesson 5.1 Counting and Writing 100 through 149

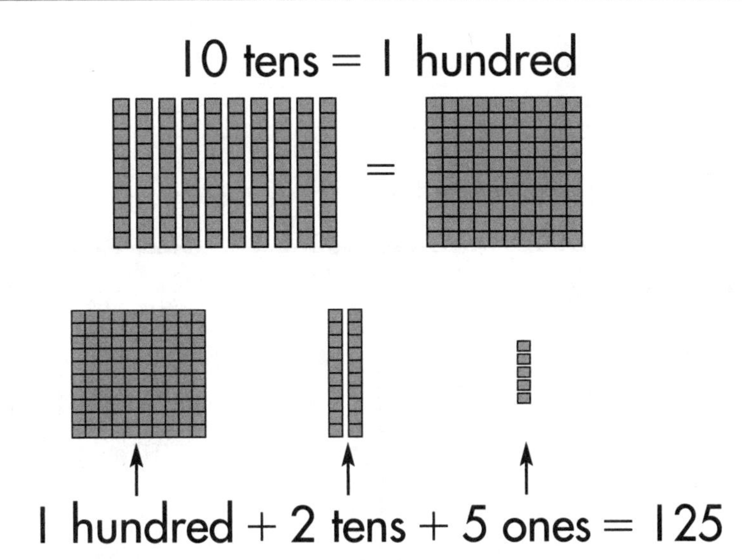

Write how many hundreds, tens, and ones.

137 = _1_ hundred _3_ tens _7_ ones

109 = ____ hundred ____ tens ____ ones

122 = ____ hundred ____ tens ____ ones

146 = ____ hundred ____ tens ____ ones

114 = ____ hundred ____ ten ____ ones

130 = ____ hundred ____ tens ____ ones

148 = ____ hundred ____ tens ____ ones

103 = ____ hundred ____ tens ____ ones

122 = ____ hundred ____ tens ____ ones

112 = ____ hundred ____ tens ____ ones

119 = ____ hundred ____ tens ____ ones

NAME ____________________

Lesson 5.2 Counting and Writing 150 through 199

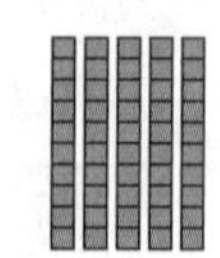

1 hundred + 5 tens + 3 ones = 153

Write the number shown.

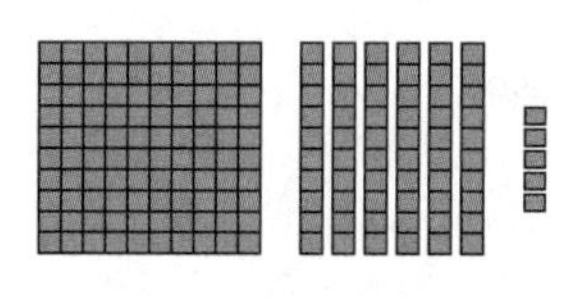

165

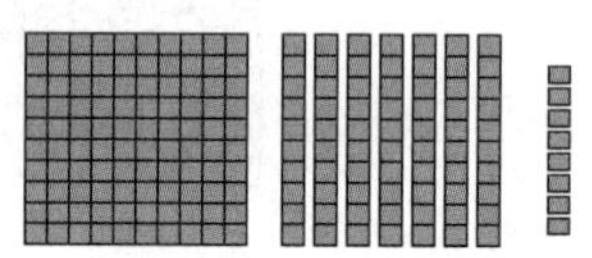

____

____

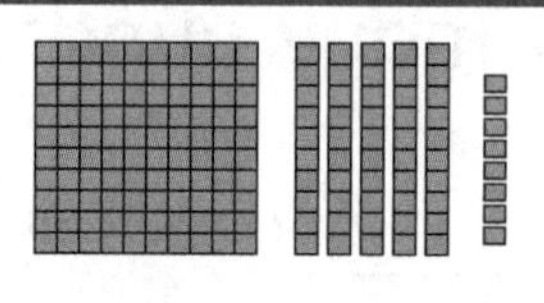

____

____

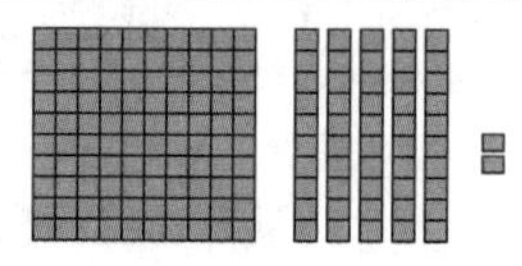

____

____

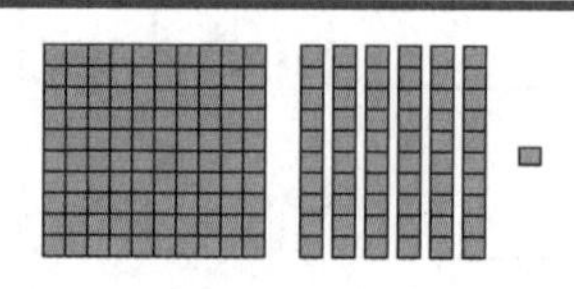

____

____

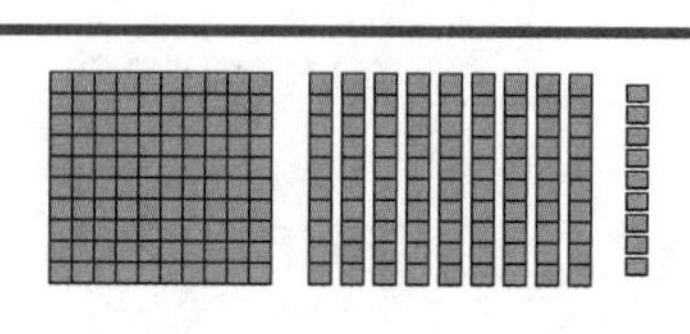

____

NAME ______________________

Lesson 5.3 Counting and Writing 200 through 399

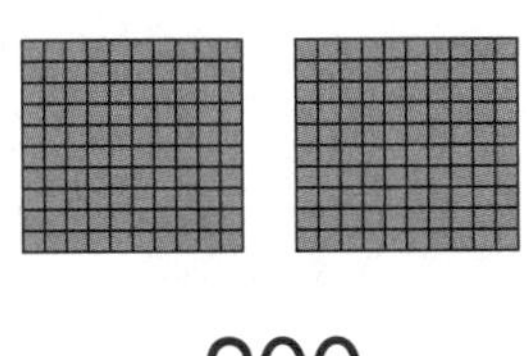

200

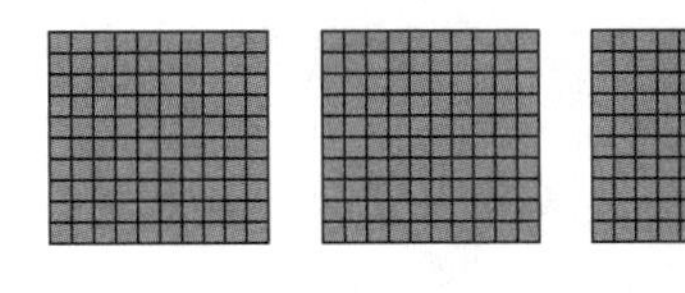

300

Write the number shown.

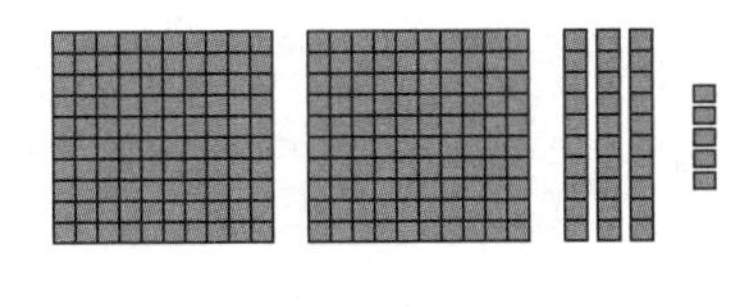

235

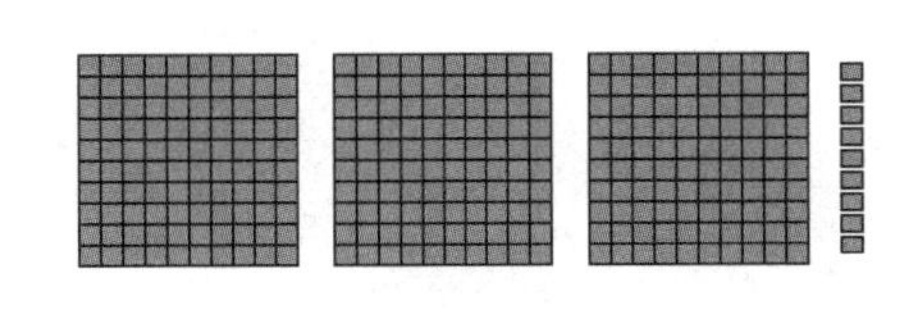

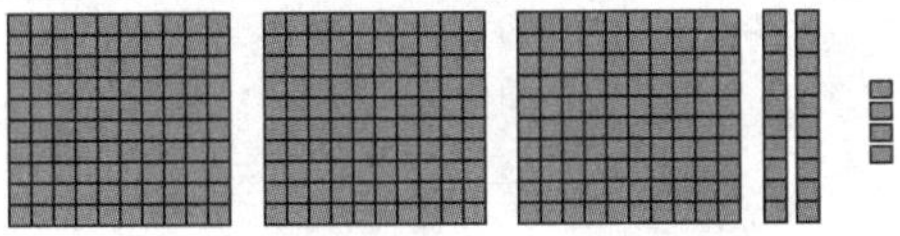

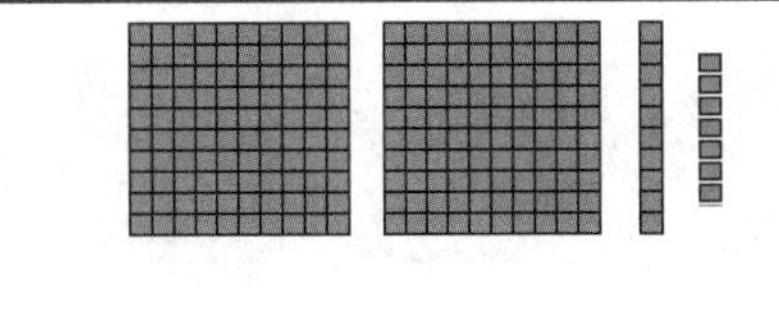

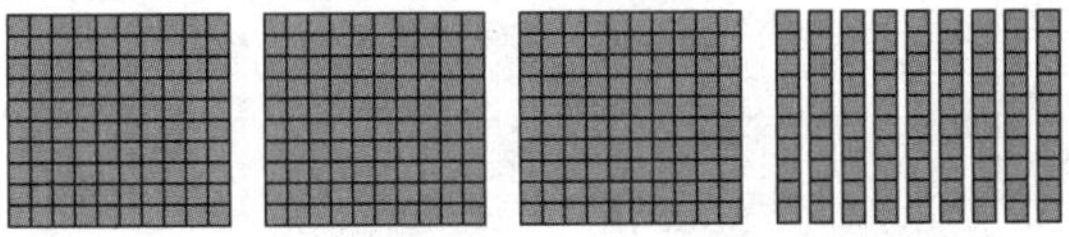

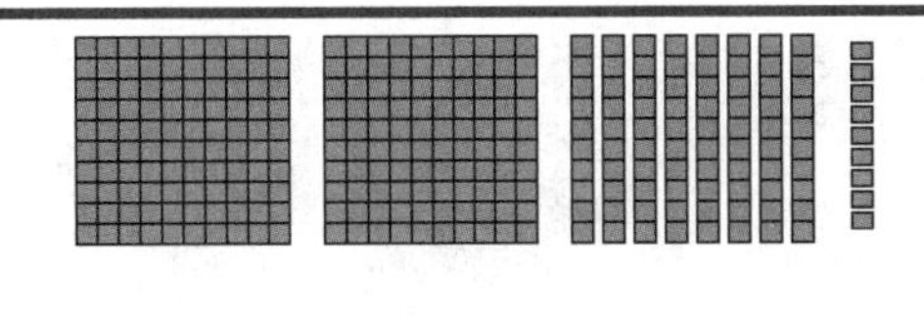

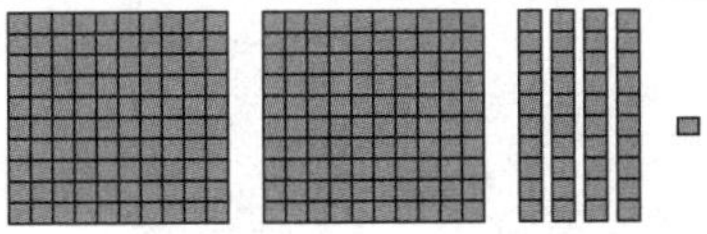

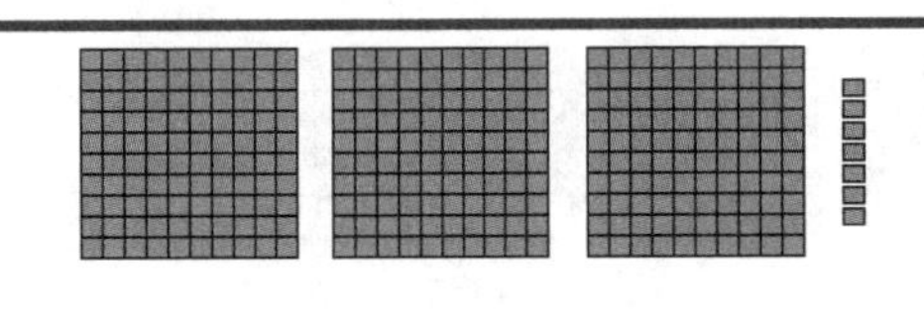

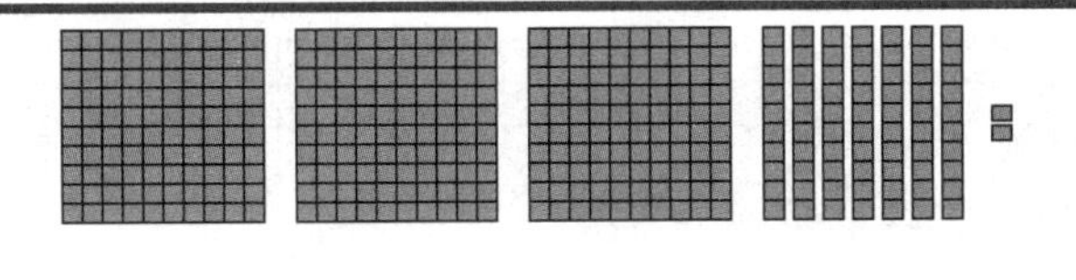

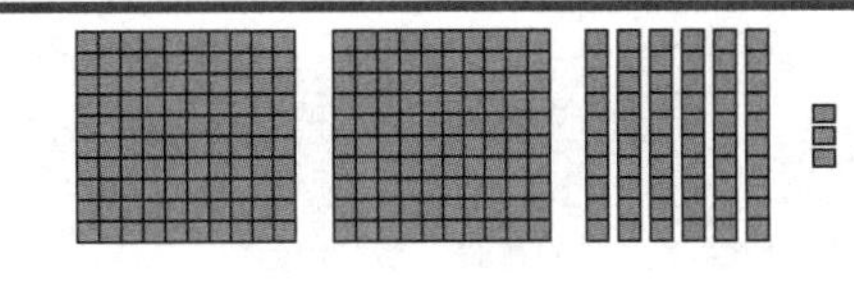

NAME ____________________

Lesson 5.4 Counting and Writing 400 through 699

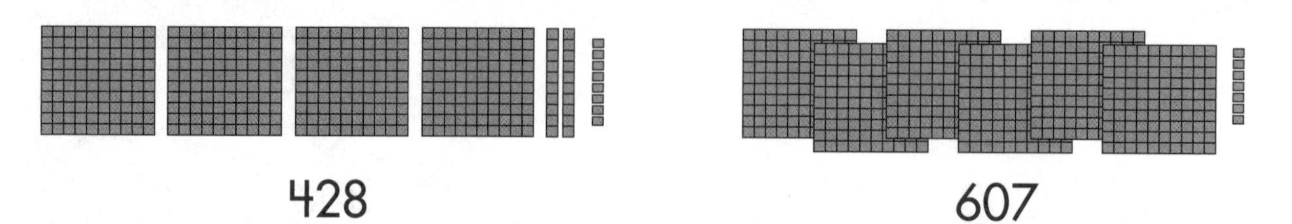

Write the number shown.

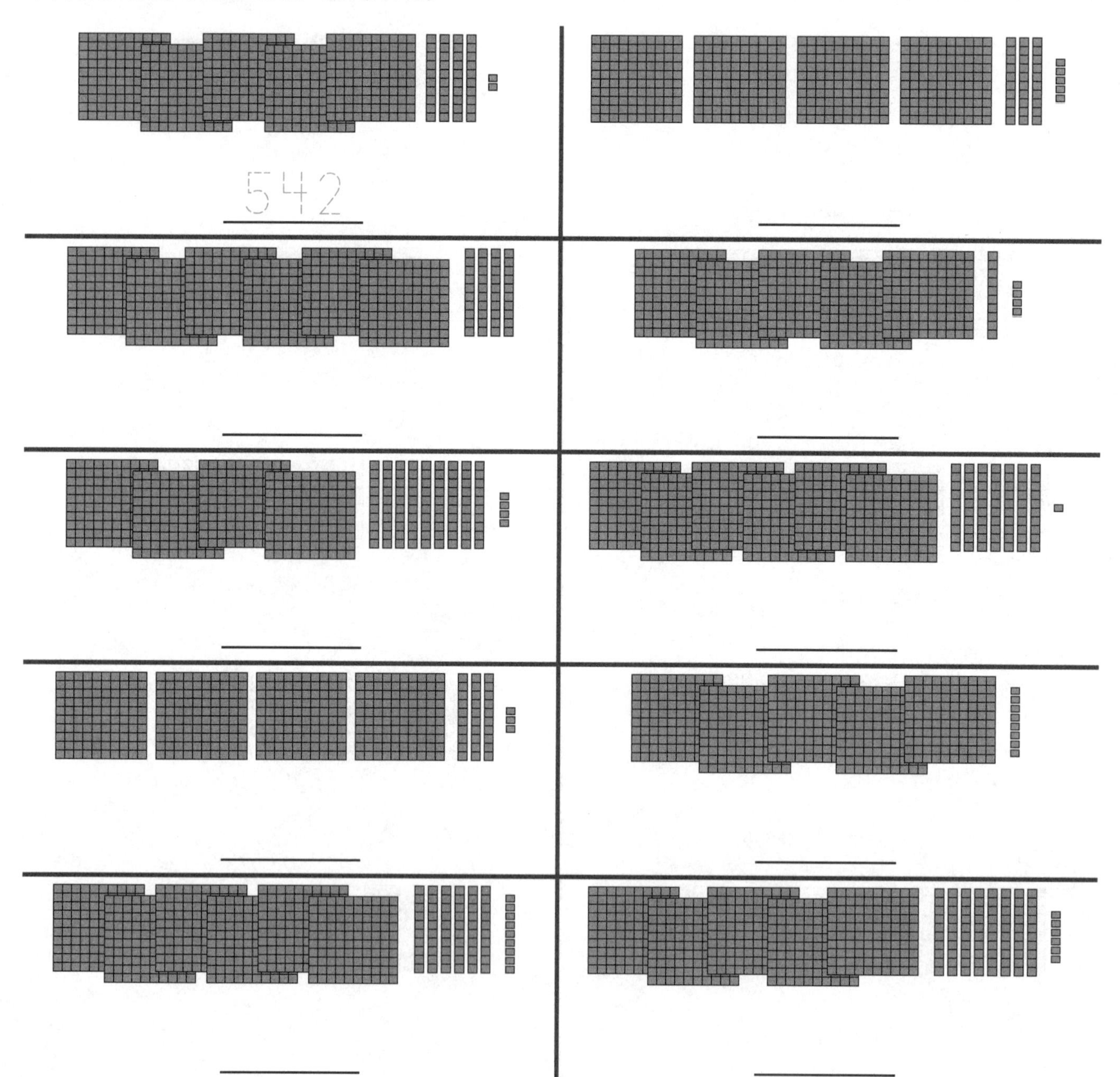

NAME ____________________

Lesson 5.5 Counting and Writing 700 through 999

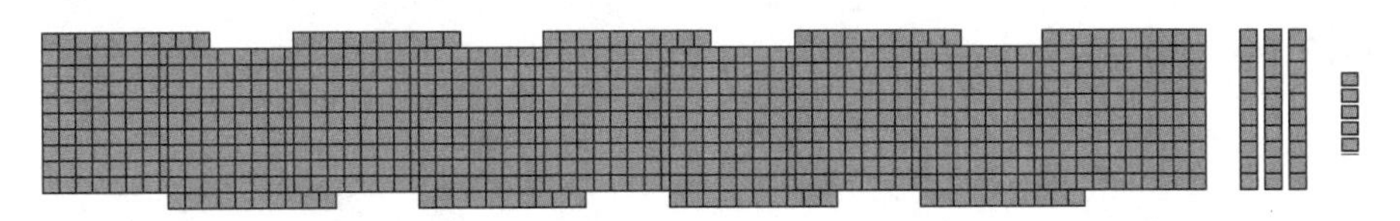

9 hundreds 3 tens 5 ones = 935

Write the number shown.

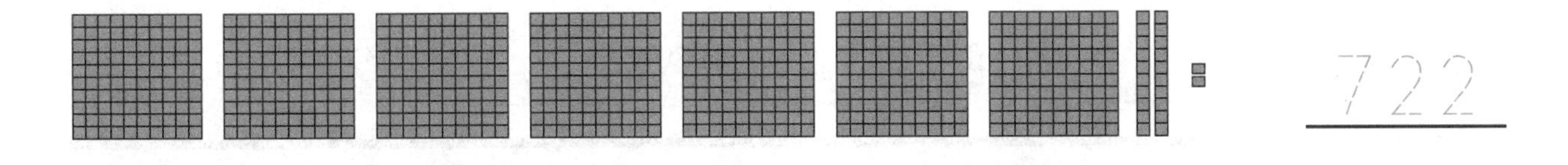

722

956

____

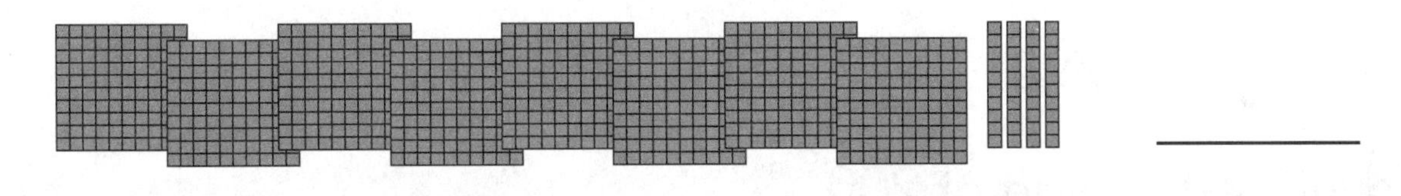

____

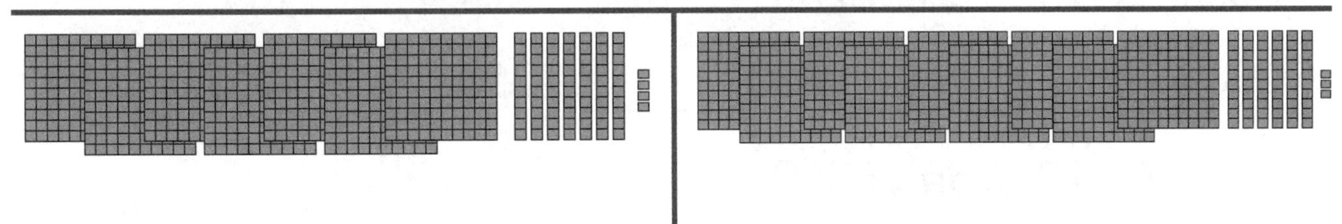

________ ________

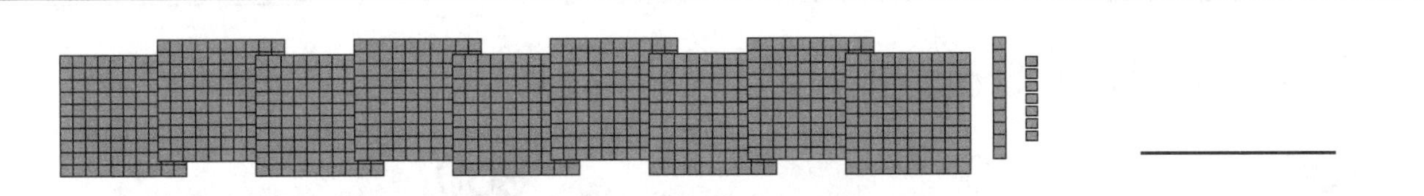

____

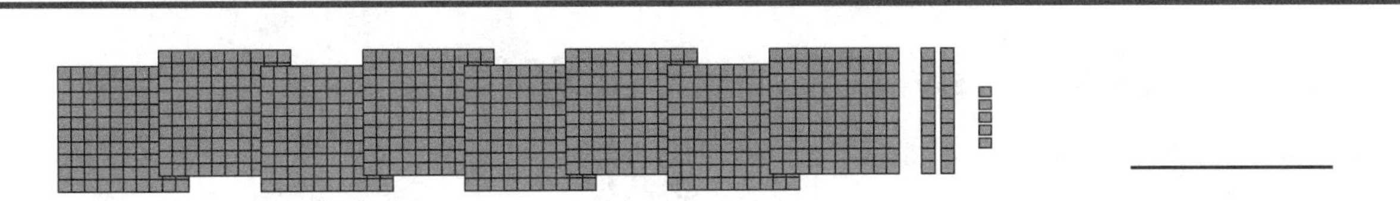

____

NAME ______________________

Lesson 5.6 Skip Counting

Count 3-digit numbers by 1.

Start at 310.

310, 311, 312, 313, 314, ______, ______, 317

Start at 415.

415, 416, 417, 418, ______, 420, ______, 422

Skip count 3-digit numbers.

Count by 5. Start at 600.

600, 605, 610, ______, ______, 625, 630, ______

Count by 5. Start at 780.

780, 785, 790, ______, 800, 805, ______, ______

Count by 10. Start at 200.

200, 210, ______, 230, ______, 250, ______, 270

Count by 10. Start at 350.

350, 360, 370, ______, ______, 400, ______, ______

Count by 100. Start at 100.

100, 200, 300, ______, ______, 600, ______

Count backward by 100. Start at 900.

900, 800, 700, ______, 500, ______, ______

NAME ______________________

Lesson 5.7 Rounding

Use the number line to round 2-digit numbers to the nearest 10.

Round *down* if ones are 4 or less.

Round *up* if ones are 5 or greater.

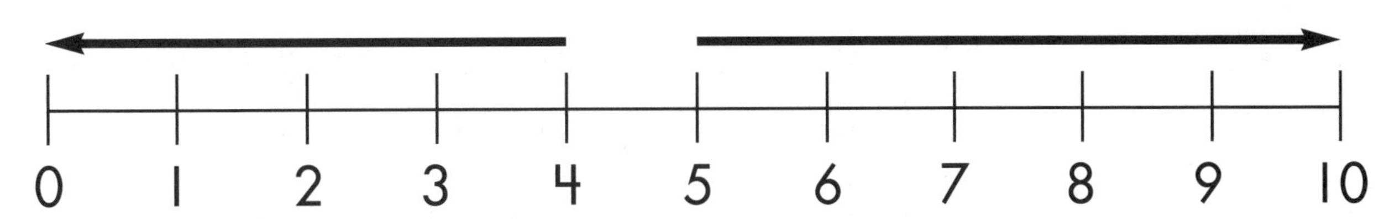

64 rounded to the nearest 10 is 60.

65 rounded to the nearest 10 is 70.

Round each number to the nearest 10.

23 20   55 60   76 ______   85 ______

37 ______   42 ______   17 ______   21 ______

83 ______   92 ______   69 ______   27 ______

51 ______   74 ______   48 ______   14 ______

94 ______   32 ______   81 ______   56 ______

63 ______   19 ______   66 ______   87 ______

43 ______   54 ______   35 ______   79 ______

13 ______   25 ______   62 ______   91 ______

73 ______   47 ______   33 ______   15 ______

Lesson 5.8 Comparing Numbers

Compare 3-digit numbers.

503	>	362	Compare hundreds. 5 is greater than 3. 503 is greater than 362.
739	<	761	If hundreds are the same, compare tens. 3 is less than 6. 739 is less than 761.
801	<	803	If hundreds and tens are the same, compare ones. 1 is less than 3. 801 is less than 803.

Compare 3-digit numbers. Use > (greater than), < (less than), or = (equal to).

831	<	843	436		379	902		911
567		564	306		401	535		535
219		198	739		730	630		820
127		119	407		610	923		925
354		453	802		792	236		401
504		504	402		408	123		118
367		562	760		740	654		736
981		901	391		491	835		830

NAME ____________________

Check What You Learned

Counting and Writing 3-Digit Numbers

Count by 1.

410, 411, ______, ______, 414, ______, ______, 417

Count by 5.

100, 105, ______, ______, 120, ______, ______, 135

560, ______, 570, ______, ______, 585, ______, 595

______, ______, 465, ______, ______, 480, ______, ______

Count by 10.

650, ______, 670, ______, ______, 700, ______, 720

900, 910, ______, ______, 940, ______, 960, ______

______, ______, 820, 830, ______, ______, 860, ______

Round each number to the nearest 10.

25 ______	83 ______	66 ______	42 ______
51 ______	37 ______	94 ______	74 ______
14 ______	46 ______	85 ______	23 ______
62 ______	58 ______	31 ______	89 ______
26 ______	91 ______	57 ______	63 ______
45 ______	12 ______	72 ______	96 ______

NAME ______________________

Check What You Learned

Counting and Writing 3-Digit Numbers

Write the number shown.

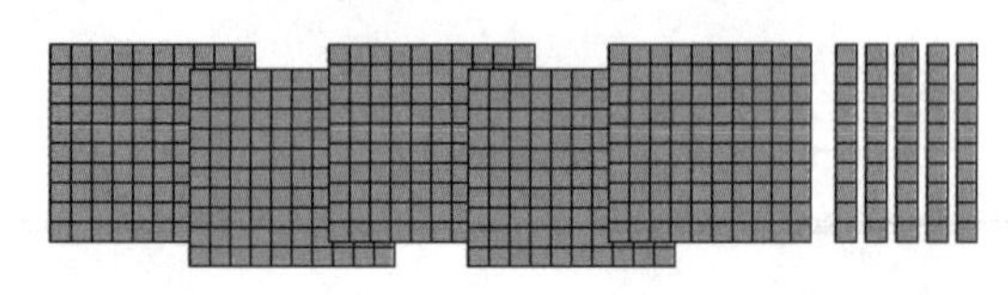

_____

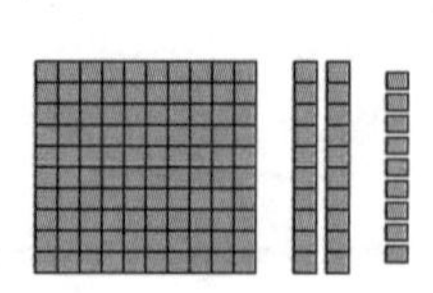

_____

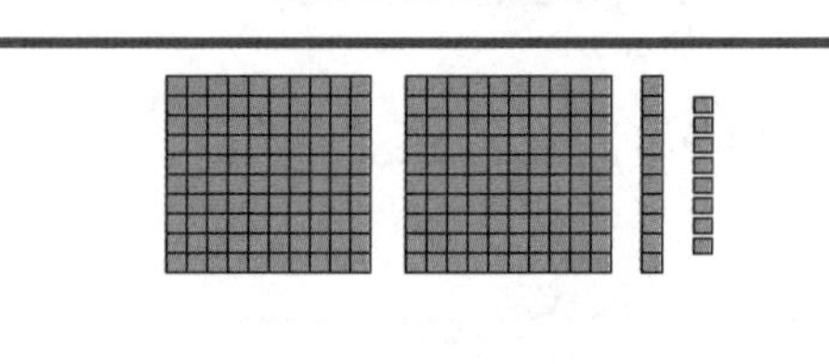

_____

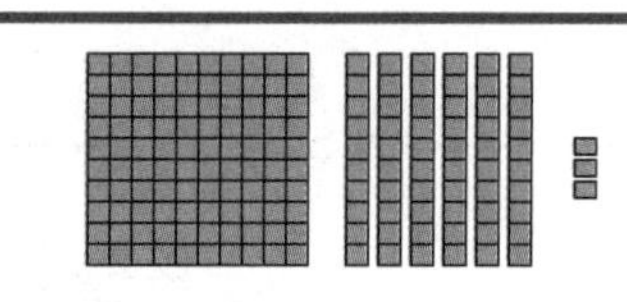

_____

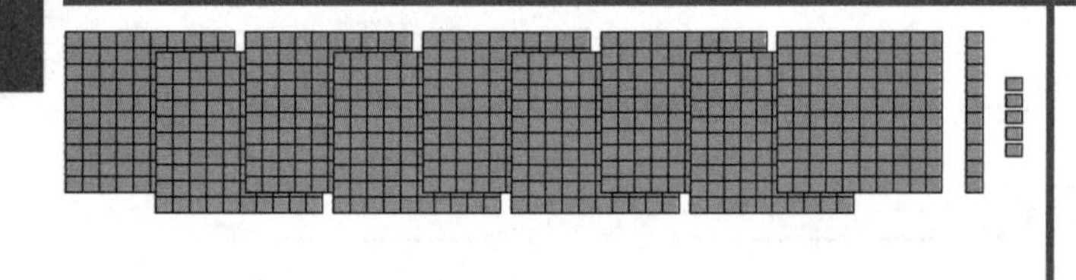

_____

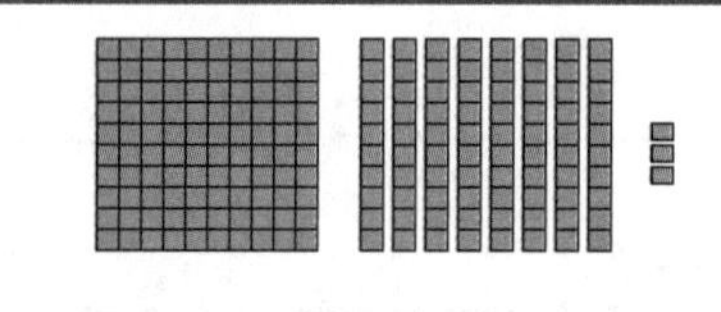

_____

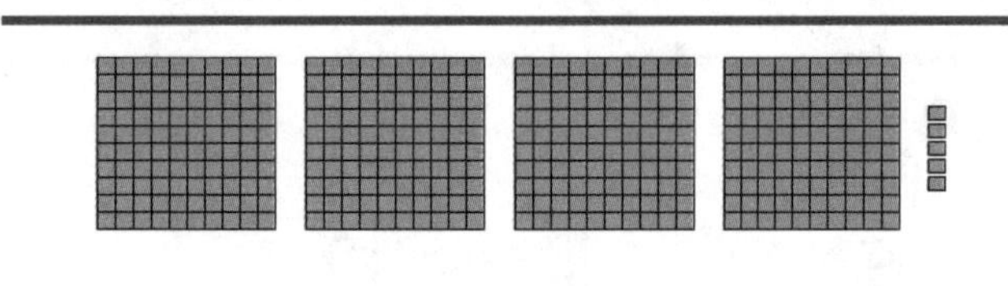

_____

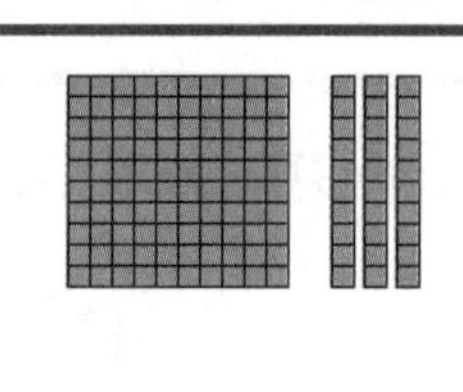

_____

Compare numbers. Use <, >, or =.

410	☐	501	653	☐	672	946	☐	942
378	☐	350	741	☐	561	143	☐	206
850	☐	796	235	☐	253	510	☐	501
910	☐	850	476	☐	476	385	☐	405

NAME ______________________

Check What You Know

Fractions

Complete.

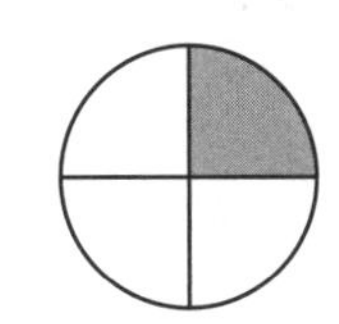

There are ______ equal parts.

______ of the parts is shaded.

______ of the shape is shaded.

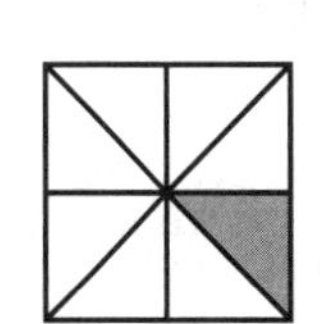

There are ______ equal parts.

______ of the parts is shaded.

______ of the shape is shaded.

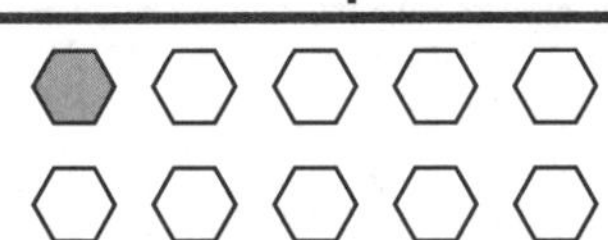

There are ______ items in the set.

______ of the items is shaded.

______ of the set is shaded.

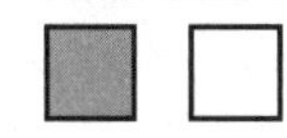

There are ______ items in the set.

______ of the items is shaded.

______ of the set is shaded.

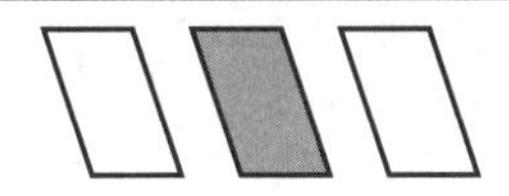

There are ______ items in the set.

______ of the items is shaded.

______ of the set is shaded.

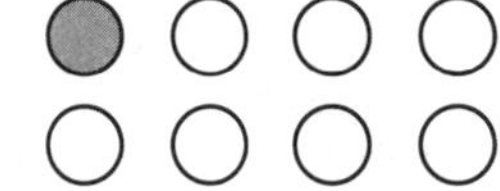

There are ______ items in the set.

______ of the items is shaded.

______ of the set is shaded.

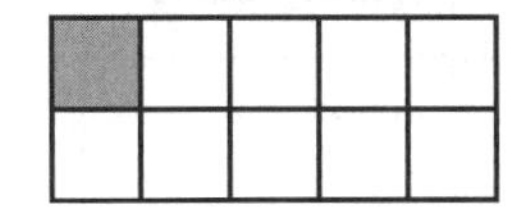

There are ______ equal parts.

______ of the parts is shaded.

______ of the shape is shaded.

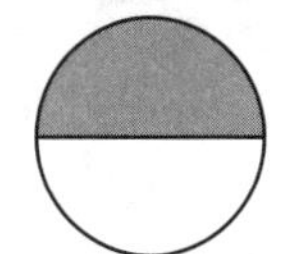

There are ______ equal parts.

______ of the parts is shaded.

______ of the shape is shaded.

NAME ______________________

Check What You Know

Fractions

Write the fraction shown. Use numbers. Then, use words.

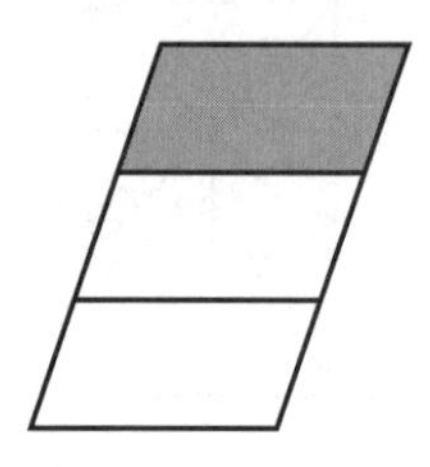

___
______, ______

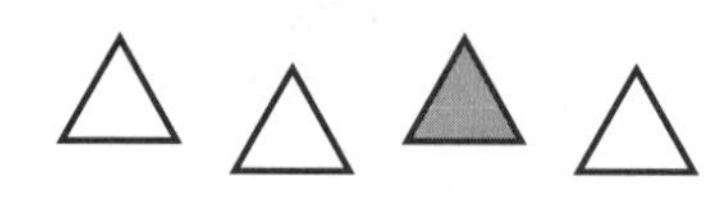

___
______, ______

___
______, ______

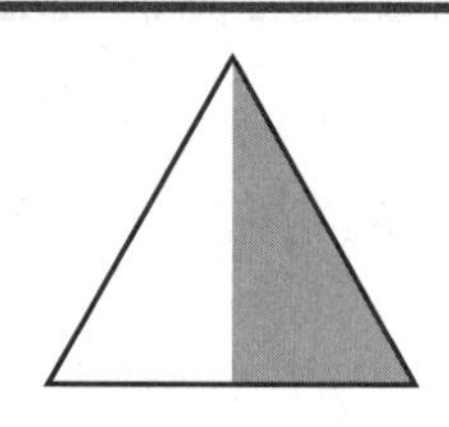

___
______, ______

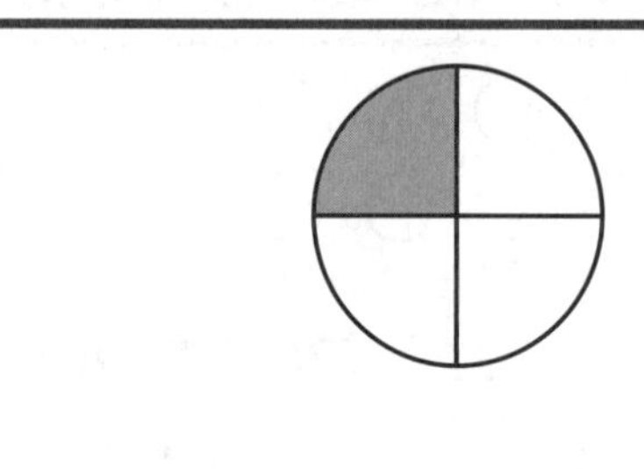

___
______, ______

___
______, ______

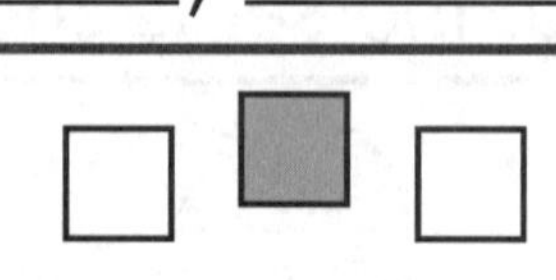

___
______, ______

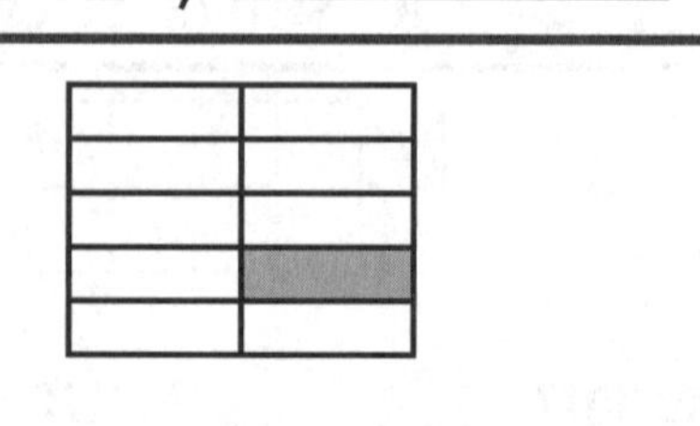

___
______, ______

NAME ____________________

Lesson 6.1 One-Half

One-half of the whole is shaded.

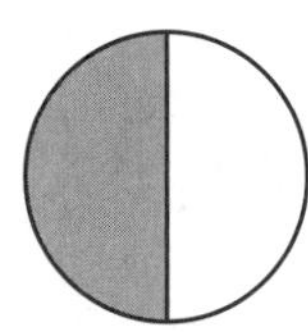

$\frac{1}{2}$ = **1** out of **2** equal parts

One-half of the set is shaded.

$\frac{1}{2}$ = **1** out of **2** items in the set

Complete.

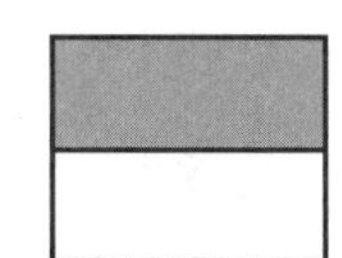

There are __2__ equal parts.

__1__ of the parts is shaded.

$\frac{1}{2}$ of the shape is shaded.

There are __2__ items in the set.

__1__ of the items is lined.

$\frac{1}{2}$ of the set is lined.

There are ______ items in the set.

______ of the items has dots.

______ of the set has dots.

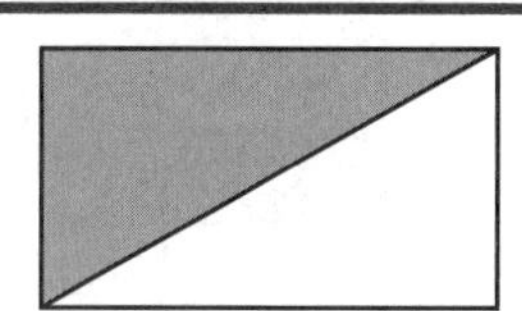

There are ______ equal parts.

______ of the parts is shaded.

______ of the shape is shaded.

Write the fraction that is shaded in words.

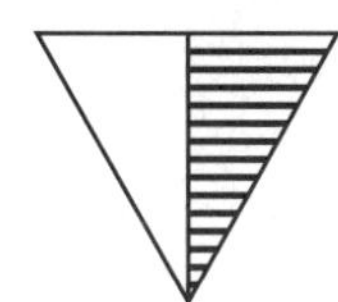

__One-half__ is shaded.

__________ is shaded.

NAME ____________________

Lesson 6.2 One-Third

One-third of the whole is shaded.

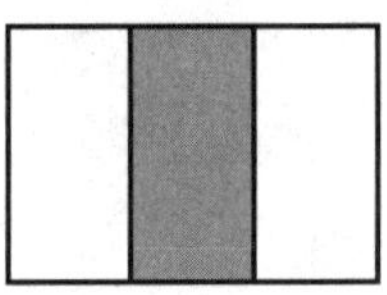

$\frac{1}{3}$ = **1** out of **3** equal parts

One-third of the set is shaded.

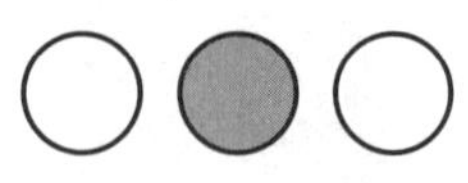

$\frac{1}{3}$ = **1** out of **3** items in the set

Complete.

There are __3__ items in the set.

__1__ of the items is lined.

$\frac{1}{3}$ of the set is lined.

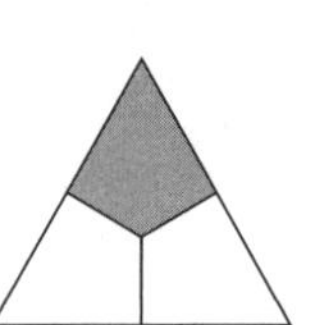

There are __3__ equal parts.

__1__ of the parts is shaded.

$\frac{1}{3}$ of the shape is shaded.

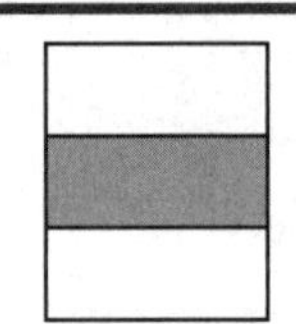

There are ______ equal parts.

______ of the parts is shaded.

______ of the shape is shaded.

There are ______ items in the set.

______ of the items has dots.

______ of the set has dots.

Write the fraction that is shaded in words.

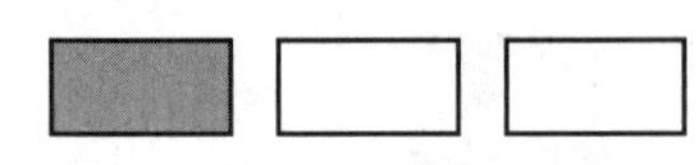

__One-third__ is shaded.

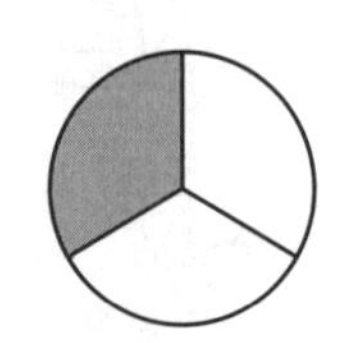

____________ is shaded.

NAME ____________________

Lesson 6.3 One-Fourth

One-fourth of the whole is shaded.

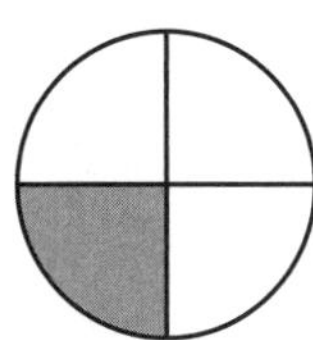

$\frac{1}{4}$ = **1** out of **4** equal parts

One-fourth of the set is shaded.

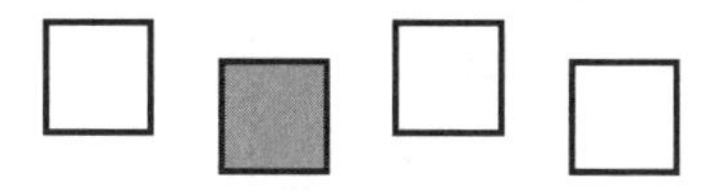

$\frac{1}{4}$ = **1** out of **4** items in the set

Complete.

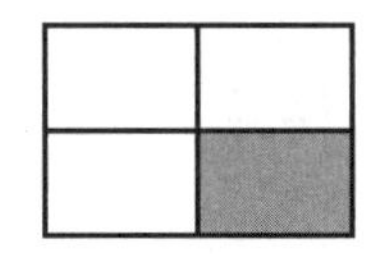

There are __4__ equal parts.

__1__ of the items is shaded.

__$\frac{1}{4}$__ of the shape is shaded.

There are ______ items in the set.

______ of the items is lined.

______ of the set is lined.

There are ______ items in the set.

______ of the items is shaded.

______ of the set is shaded.

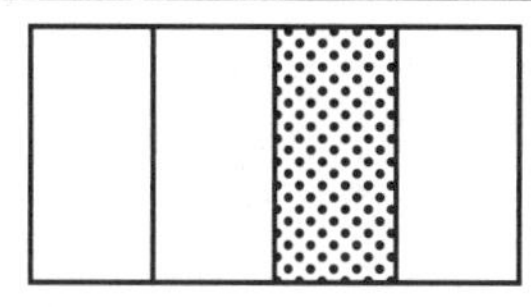

There are ______ equal parts.

______ of the parts has dots.

______ of the shape has dots.

Write the fraction that is shaded in words.

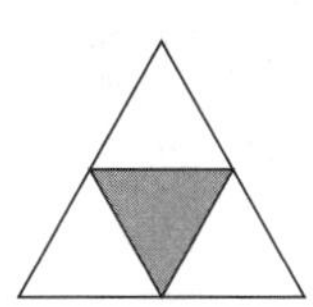

__One-fourth__ is shaded.

__________ is shaded.

NAME ____________________

Lesson 6.4 One-Eighth

One-eighth of the whole is shaded.

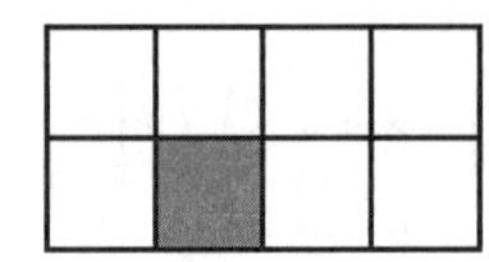

$\frac{1}{8}$ = **1** out of **8** equal parts

One-eighth of the set is shaded.

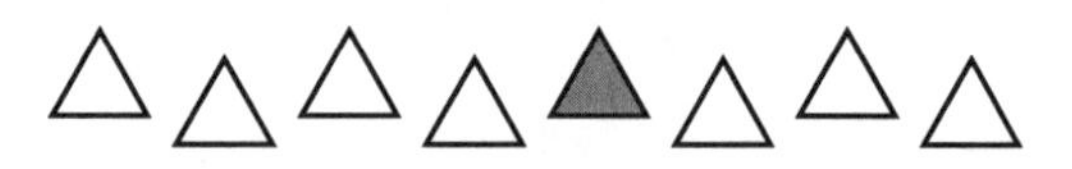

$\frac{1}{8}$ = **1** out of **8** items in the set

Complete.

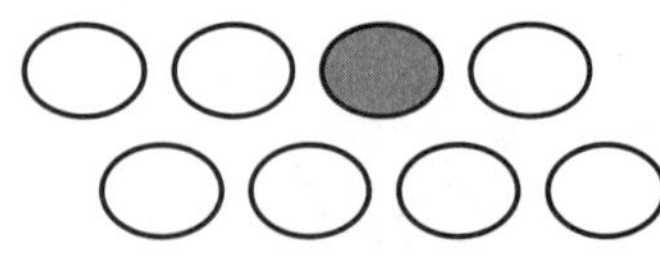

There are __8__ items in the set.

__1__ of the items is shaded.

__$\frac{1}{8}$__ of the set is shaded.

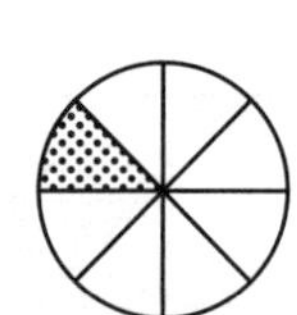

There are ______ equal parts.

______ of the parts has dots.

______ of the shape has dots.

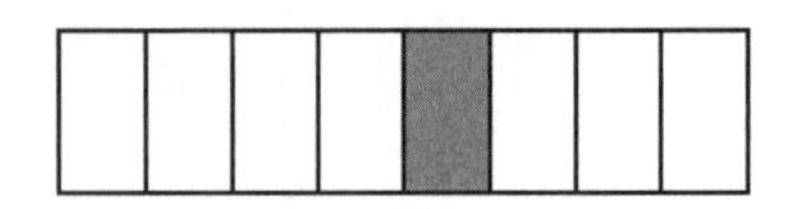

There are ______ equal parts.

______ of the parts is shaded.

______ of the shape is shaded.

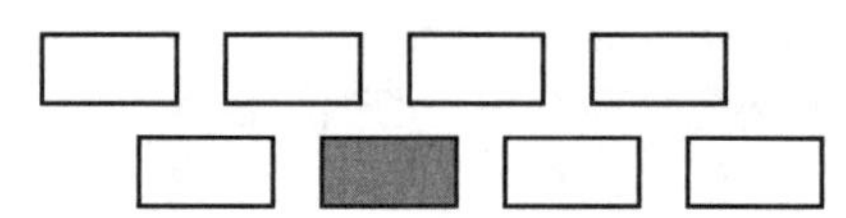

There are ______ items in the set.

______ of the items is shaded.

______ of the set is shaded.

Write the fraction that is shaded in words.

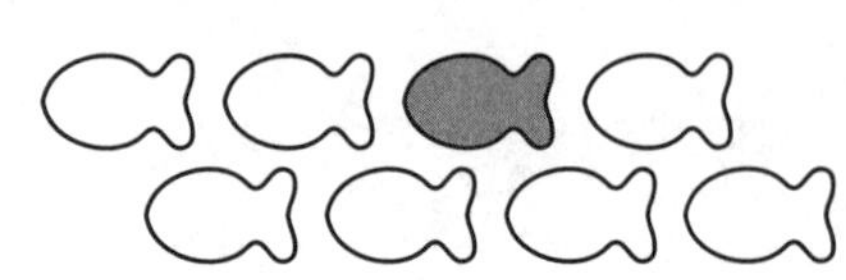

__One-eighth__ is shaded.

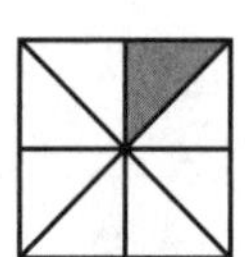

__________ is shaded.

NAME ____________________

Lesson 6.5 One-Tenth

One-tenth of the whole is shaded.

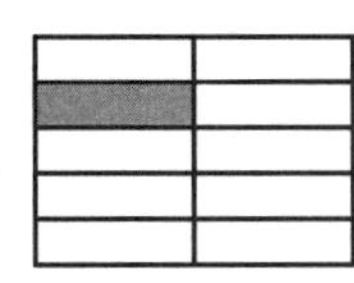

$\frac{1}{10}$ = **1** out of **10** equal parts

One-tenth of the set is shaded.

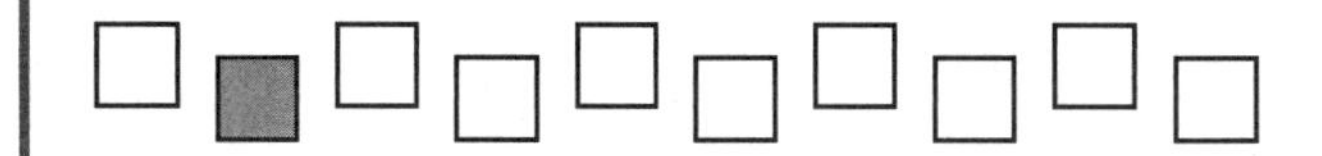

$\frac{1}{10}$ = **1** out of **10** items in the set

Complete.

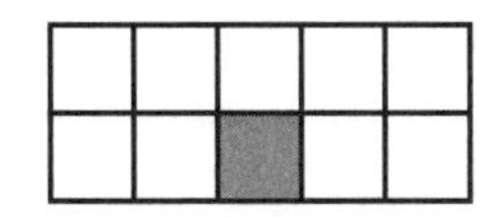

There are <u>10</u> equal parts.

<u>1</u> of the parts is shaded.

$\frac{1}{10}$ of the shape is shaded.

There are ______ items in the set.

______ of the items is shaded.

______ of the set is shaded.

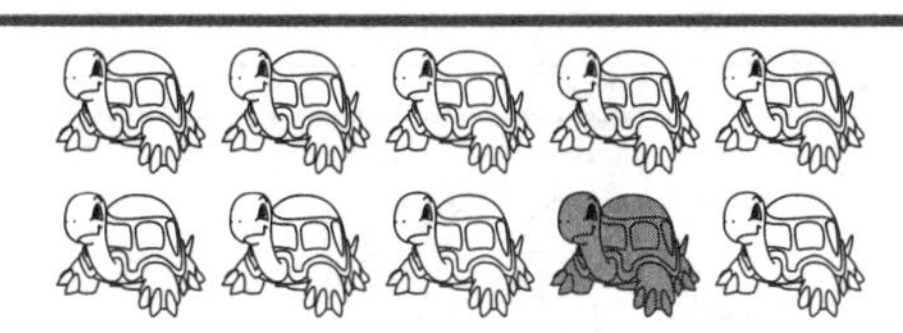

There are ______ items in the set.

______ of the items is shaded.

______ of the set is shaded.

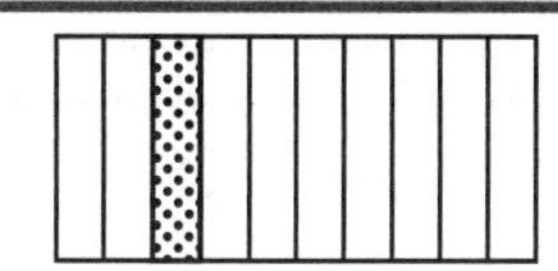

There are ______ equal parts.

______ of the parts has dots.

______ of the shape has dots.

Write the fraction that is shaded in words.

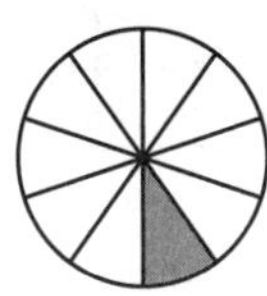

<u>One-tenth</u> is shaded.

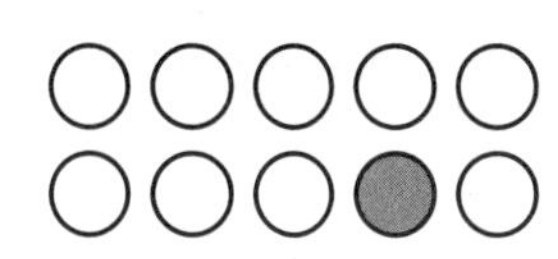

__________ is shaded.

NAME ____________________

Lesson 6.6 Identifying Fractions

What fraction is shown?
Think: How many of the items are shaded?
How many items are in the set?

$\frac{1}{4}$

What fraction is shown?
Think: How many of the parts are shaded?
How many equal parts?

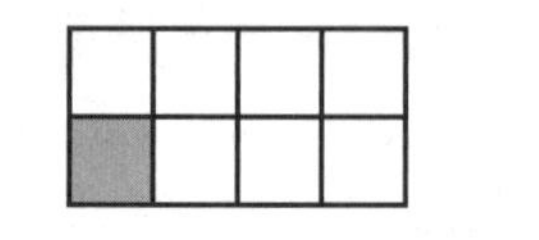

$\frac{1}{8}$

Write the fraction shown. Use numbers. Then, use words.

$\frac{1}{3}$, one-third

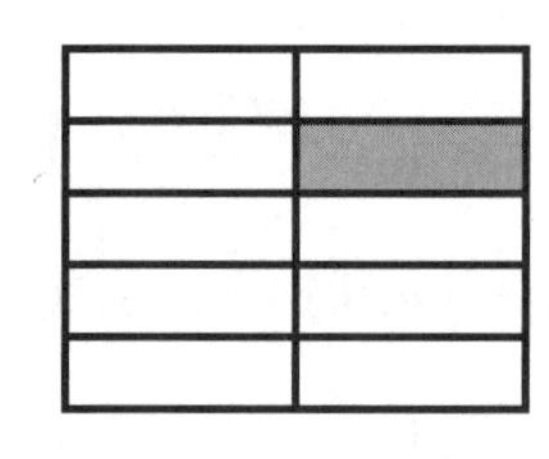

—
____, ________

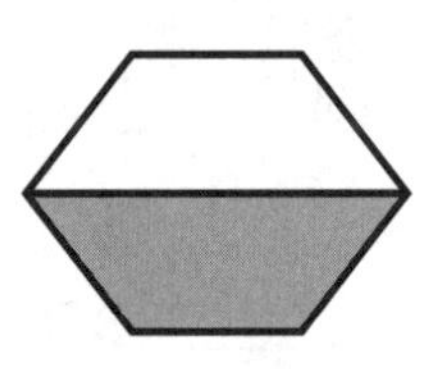

—
____, ________

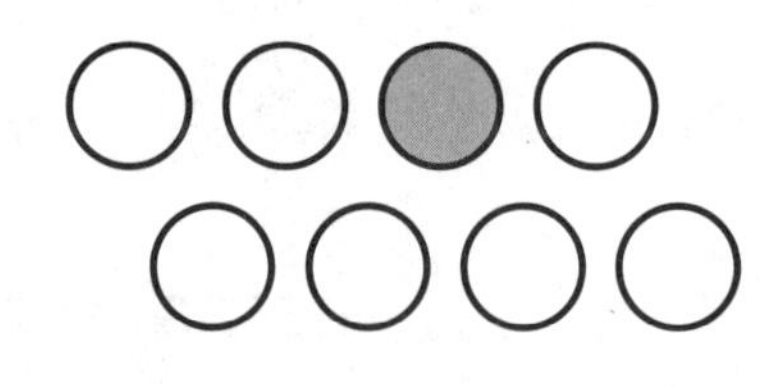

—
____, ________

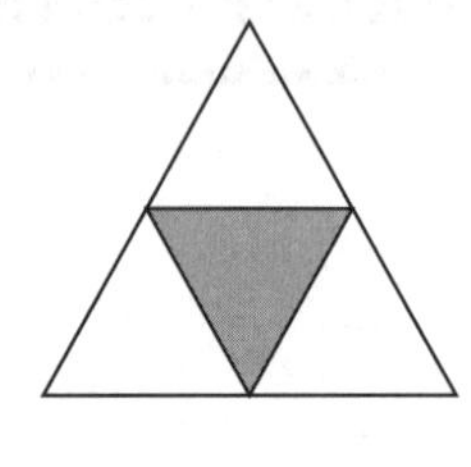

—
____, ________

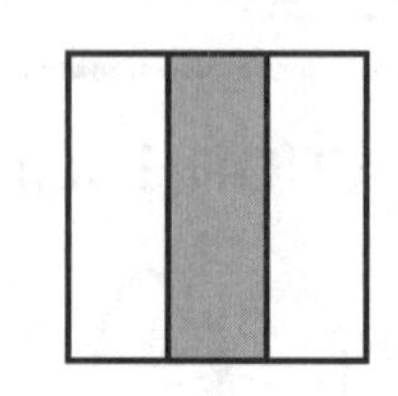

—
____, ________

NAME ______________________

Check What You Learned

Fractions

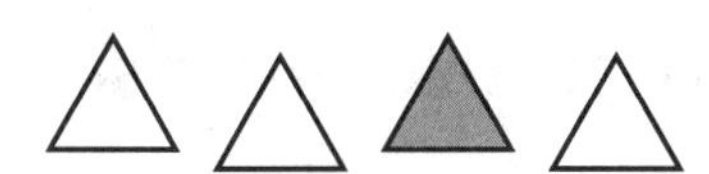

There are ______ items in the set.

______ of the items is shaded.

______ of the set is shaded.

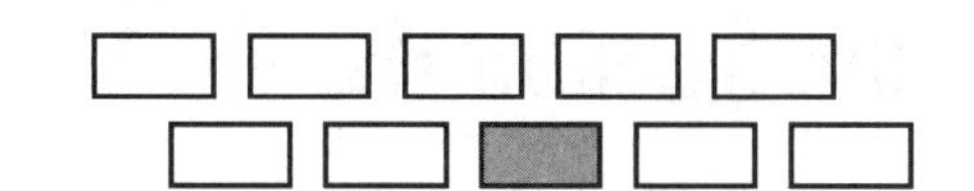

There are ______ items in the set.

______ of the items is shaded.

______ of the set is shaded.

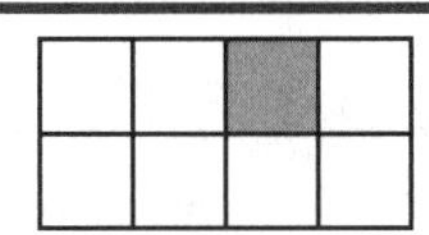

There are ______ equal parts.

______ of the parts is shaded.

______ of the shape is shaded.

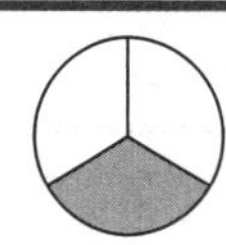

There are ______ equal parts.

______ of the parts is shaded.

______ of the shape is shaded.

There are ______ items in the set.

______ of the items is shaded.

______ of the set is shaded.

There are ______ items in the set.

______ of the items is shaded.

______ of the set is shaded.

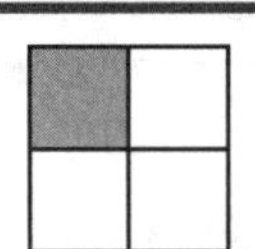

There are ______ equal parts.

______ of the parts is shaded.

______ of the shape is shaded.

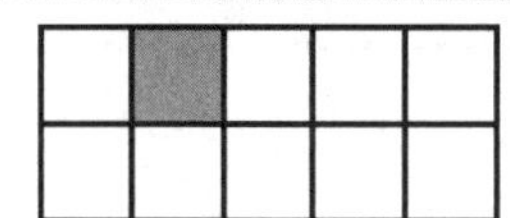

There are ______ equal parts.

______ of the parts is shaded.

______ of the shape is shaded.

NAME ________________________

Check What You Learned

Fractions

Write the fraction shown. Use numbers. Then, use words.

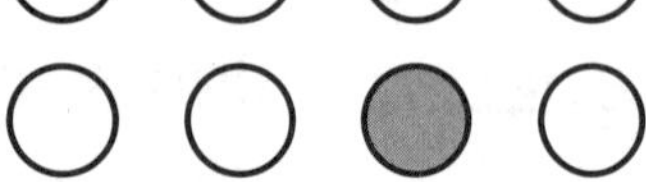

___ , ________

___ , ________

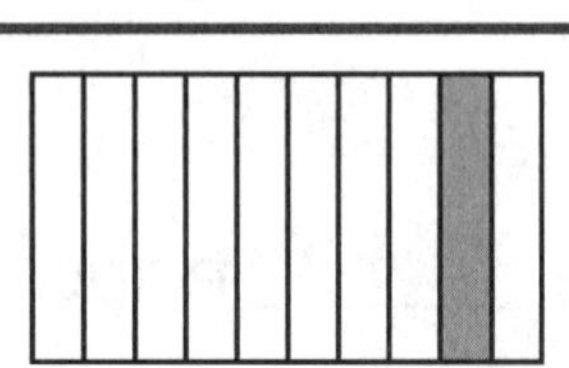
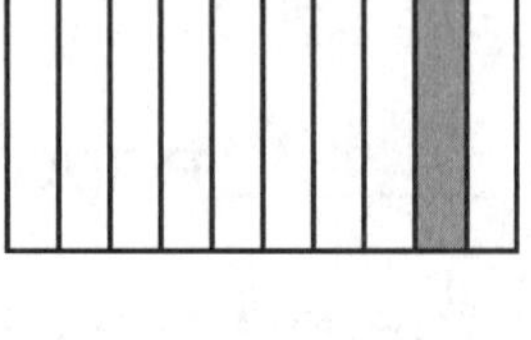

___ , ________

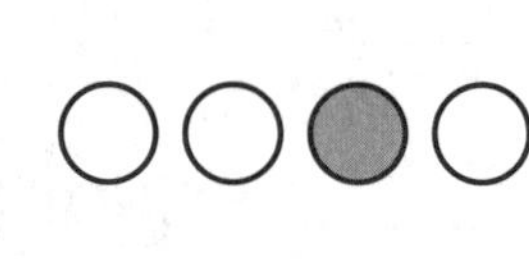

___ , ________

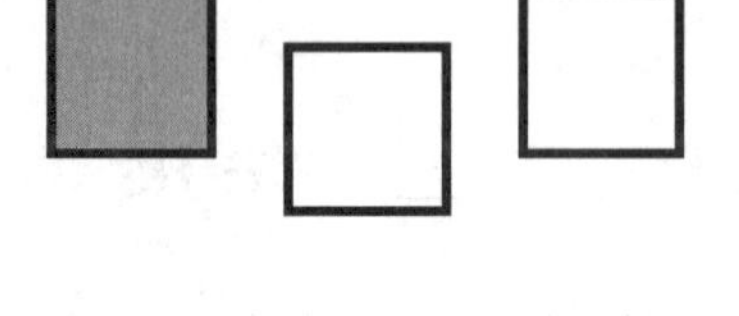

___ , ________

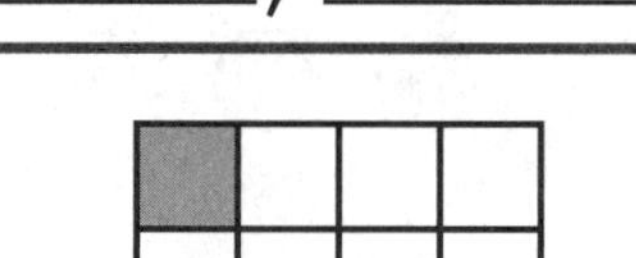

___ , ________

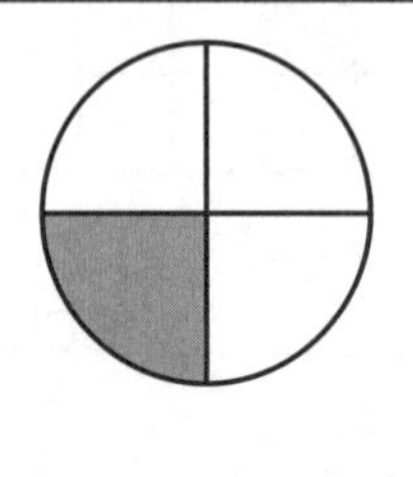

___ , ________

___ , ________

NAME ____________________

Check What You Know

Measurement

Use an inch ruler. Measure each object.

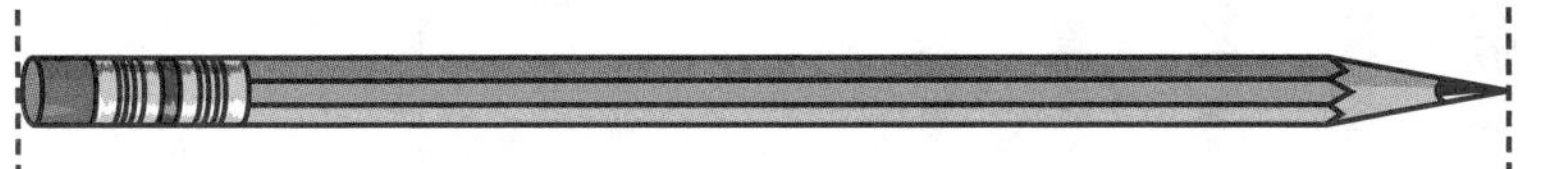

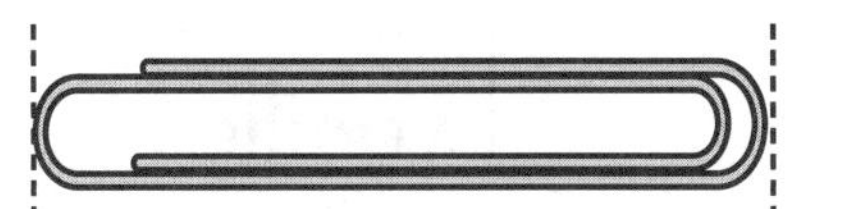

_____ inches   _____ inches

This is one square unit ☐. What is the area of the figure?

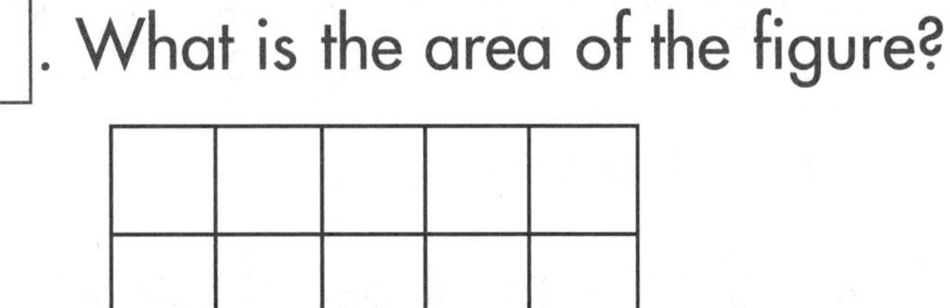

_____ square units

Tell the time on each clock.

____ : ____   _____ o'clock   ____ : ____

Use the calendar to answer the questions.

How many days are in this month? _________

How many Mondays are in this month? _________

September						
Sun.	Mon.	Tues.	Wed.	Thurs.	Fri.	Sat.
				1	2	3
4	5	6	7	8	9	10
11	12	13	14	15	16	17
18	19	20	21	22	23	24
25	26	27	28	29	30	

NAME ____________________

Check What You Know

Measurement

Favorite Ice Cream Flavors

Vanilla	
Chocolate	
Cookie Dough	

= 1 person

Which flavor did the most people pick? ____________

How many people chose chocolate? ______

How many people chose either vanilla or chocolate? ______

Add the number of cents shown.

¢

\+ ______ ¢

¢

¢

\+ ______ ¢

¢

Read the temperature in °F and °C. Round °F to the nearest 10.

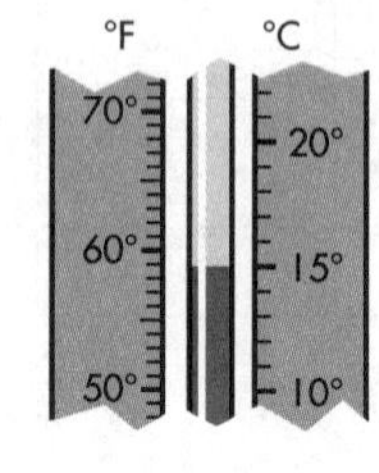

______ °F ______ °C

Circle the correct words.

is greater than

is equal to

is less than

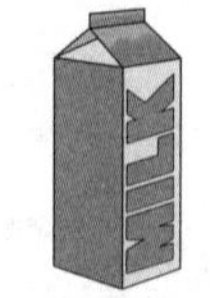

2 pints

1 quart

NAME ______________________

Lesson 7.1 Money

nickel	dime	quarter	half-dollar

5¢	10¢	25¢	50¢

Add the number of cents shown.

20¢
+ 50¢
70¢

¢
+ ¢
¢

¢
+ ¢
¢

¢
+ ¢
¢

¢
¢
+ ¢
¢

¢

¢

+ ¢
¢

Lesson 7.1 Money

What is the value of each group of coins?

is greater than

is less than (circled)

is equal to

65 ¢ ______ 70 ¢

Find the value of each set of coins. Circle the correct words.

is greater than

is less than

is equal to

______ ¢ ______ ¢

is greater than

is less than

is equal to

______ ¢ ______ ¢

is greater than

is less than

is equal to

______ ¢ ______ ¢

is greater than

is less than

is equal to

______ ¢ ______ ¢

is greater than

is less than

is equal to

______ ¢ ______ ¢

NAME ____________________

Lesson 7.2 Telling Time to the Hour

4 o'clock
4:00

Both clocks show 4 o'clock, or 4:00.

Write the time two ways.

 7 o'clock 7:00	 ____ o'clock ____:____	 ____ o'clock ____:____
 ____ o'clock ____:____	 ____ o'clock ____:____	 ____ o'clock ____:____
 ____ o'clock ____:____	 ____ o'clock ____:____	 ____ o'clock ____:____

NAME ______________________

Lesson 7.3 Telling Time to the Half Hour

7 o'clock
7:00

half past 7
7:30

8 o'clock
8:00

Write the time two ways.

half past 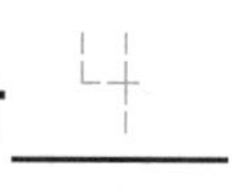

4:30

10:30

half past ____

____ : ____

half past ____

____ : ____

half past ____

____ : ____

half past ____

____ : ____

half past ____

____ : ____

half past ____

____ : ____

half past ____

____ : ____

half past ____

____ : ____

NAME ______________________

Lesson 7.4 Telling Time to the Quarter Hour

1:15
one fifteen

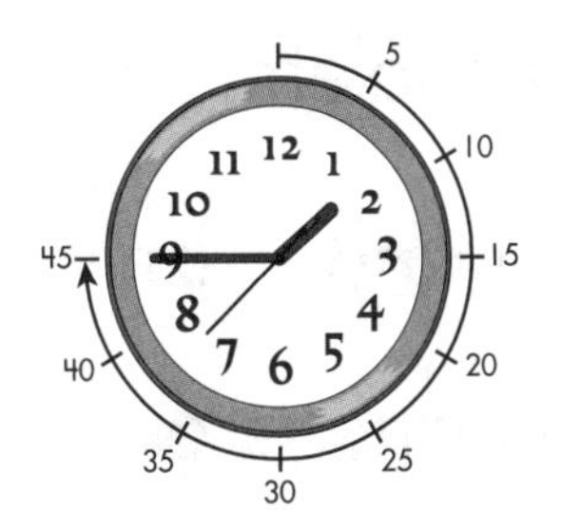

1:45
one forty-five

Read the time on the first clock.
Write the same time on the second clock.

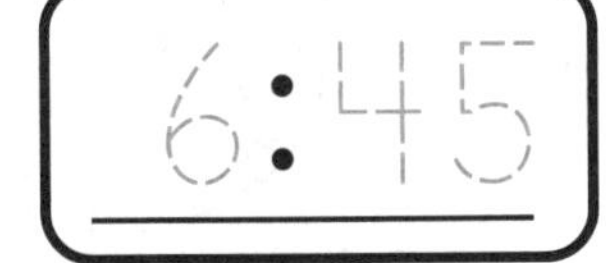

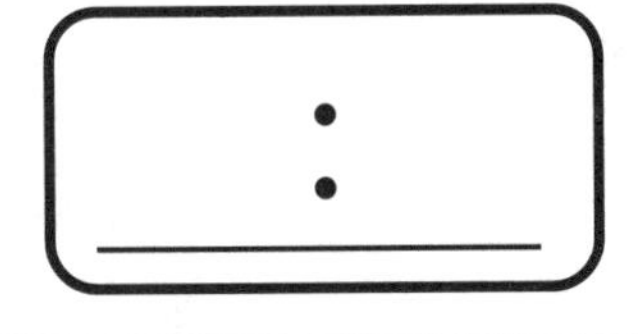

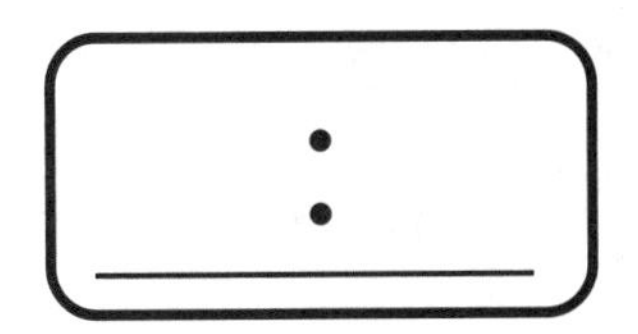

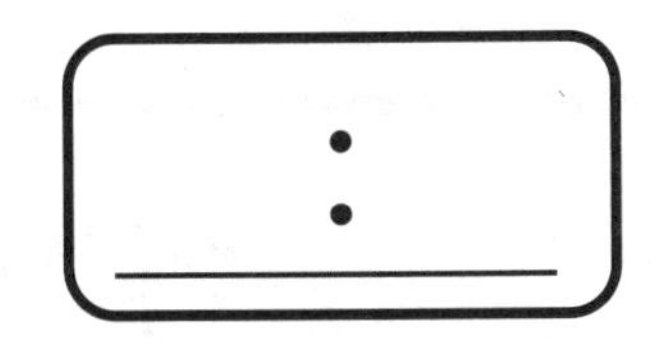

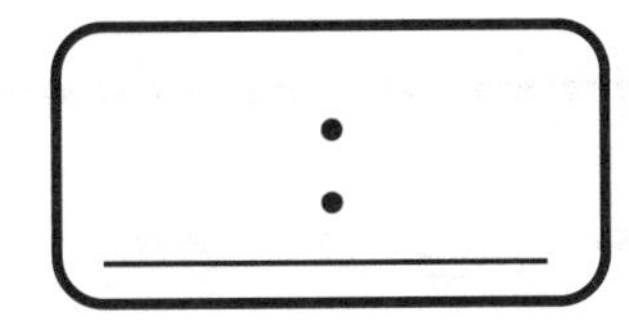

NAME ____________________

Lesson 7.4 Problem Solving

Solve each problem.

The small hand is between 3 and 4.

The large hand is on the 6.

The time is 3:30.

The small hand is between ____ and ____.

The large hand is on the ____.

The time is ___:___.

The small hand is on the ____.

The large hand is on the ____.

The time is ___:___.

The small hand is between ____ and ____.

The large hand is on the ____.

The time is ___:___.

The small hand is on the ____.

The large hand is on the ____.

The time is ___:___.

NAME ____________________

Lesson 7.5 Reading the Calendar

This calendar shows one month.

The letters at the top of the calendar stand for the days of the week:

Sunday, Monday, Tuesday, Wednesday, Thursday, Friday, and Saturday.

Use the calendar to answer the questions.

March						
S	M	T	W	Th	F	Sa
		1	2	3	4	5
6	7	8	9	10	11	12
13	14	15	16	17	18	19
20	21	22	23	24	25	26
27	28	29	30	31		

On what day of the week does this month begin? Tuesday

How many days are in this month? __________

How many Sundays are in this month? __________

How many Wednesdays are in this month? __________

What day of the week is the 18th? __________

How many days are in 2 weeks? __________

NAME ____________________

Lesson 7.5 Reading the Calendar

This calendar shows one year. A year is 365 days.

The letters at the top of the calendar stand for the days of the week:

Sunday, Monday, Tuesday, Wednesday, Thursday, Friday, Saturday.

Use the calendar to answer the questions.

January

S	M	T	W	T	F	S
						1
2	3	4	5	6	7	8
9	10	11	12	13	14	15
16	17	18	19	20	21	22
23	24	25	26	27	28	29
30	31					

February

S	M	T	W	T	F	S
		1	2	3	4	5
6	7	8	9	10	11	12
13	14	15	16	17	18	19
20	21	22	23	24	25	26
27	28					

March

S	M	T	W	T	F	S
		1	2	3	4	5
6	7	8	9	10	11	12
13	14	15	16	17	18	19
20	21	22	23	24	25	26
27	28	29	30	31		

April

S	M	T	W	T	F	S
					1	2
3	4	5	6	7	8	9
10	11	12	13	14	15	16
17	18	19	20	21	22	23
24	25	26	27	28	29	30

May

S	M	T	W	T	F	S
1	2	3	4	5	6	7
8	9	10	11	12	13	14
15	16	17	18	19	20	21
22	23	24	25	26	27	28
29	30	31				

June

S	M	T	W	T	F	S
			1	2	3	4
5	6	7	8	9	10	11
12	13	14	15	16	17	18
19	20	21	22	23	24	25
26	27	28	29	30		

July

S	M	T	W	T	F	S
					1	2
3	4	5	6	7	8	9
10	11	12	13	14	15	16
17	18	19	20	21	22	23
24	25	26	27	28	29	30
31						

August

S	M	T	W	T	F	S
	1	2	3	4	5	6
7	8	9	10	11	12	13
14	15	16	17	18	19	20
21	22	23	24	25	26	27
28	29	30	31			

September

S	M	T	W	T	F	S
				1	2	3
4	5	6	7	8	9	10
11	12	13	14	15	16	17
18	19	20	21	22	23	24
25	26	27	28	29	30	

October

S	M	T	W	T	F	S
						1
2	3	4	5	6	7	8
9	10	11	12	13	14	15
16	17	18	19	20	21	22
23	24	25	26	27	28	29
30	31					

November

S	M	T	W	T	F	S
		1	2	3	4	5
6	7	8	9	10	11	12
13	14	15	16	17	18	19
20	21	22	23	24	25	26
27	28	29	30			

December

S	M	T	W	T	F	S
				1	2	3
4	5	6	7	8	9	10
11	12	13	14	15	16	17
18	19	20	21	22	23	24
25	26	27	28	29	30	31

How many days are in one week? ____

How many months are in one year? ________

Which month has 28 days? ________

Which months have 30 days? ________, ________,

________, ________

What is the first month of the year? ________

What is the last month of the year? ________

Lesson 7.6 Measuring Length in Inches

This is 1 inch.

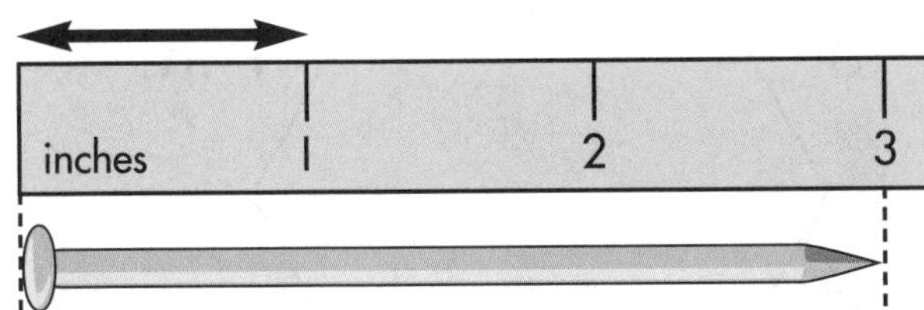

The nail is 3 inches long.

Write the length of each object in inches.

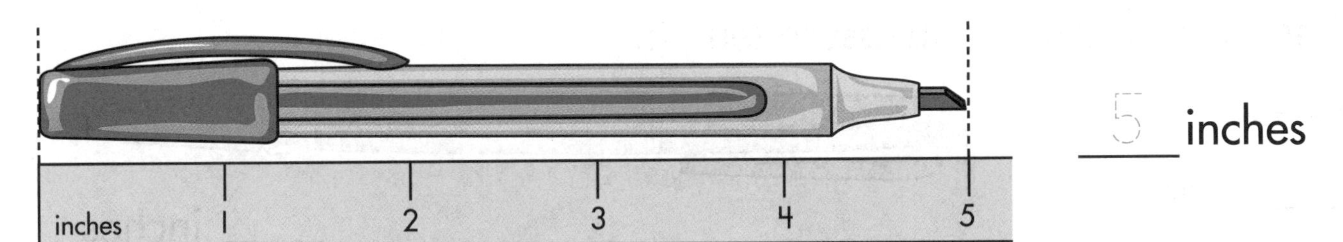

5 inches

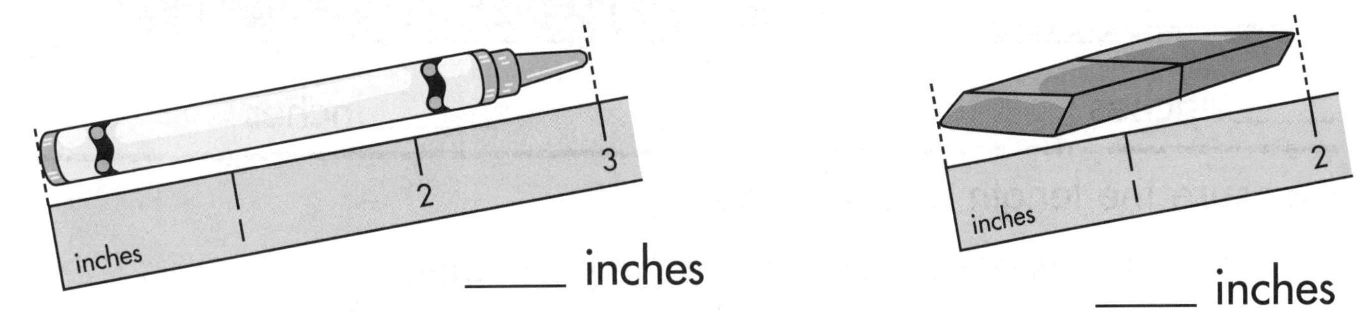

_____ inches

_____ inches

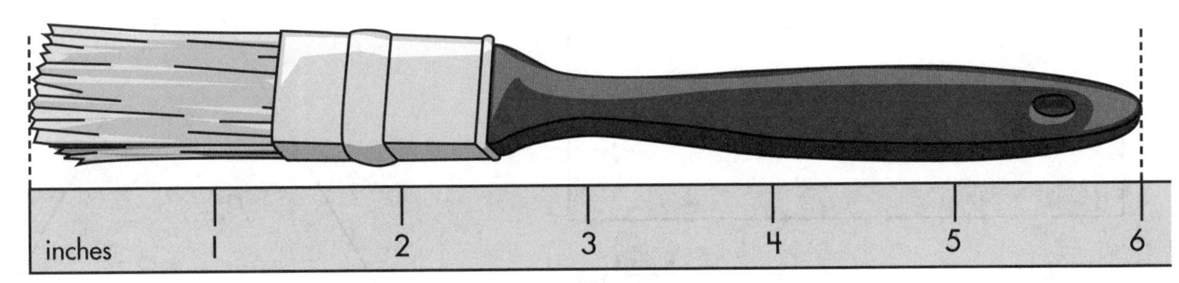

_____ inches

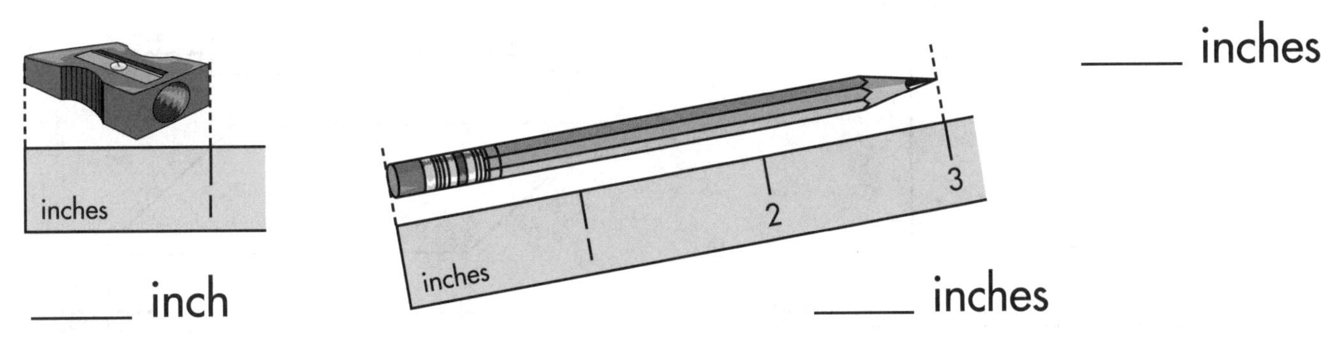

_____ inch

_____ inches

NAME ___________________________

Lesson 7.6 Measuring Length in Inches

Perimeter is the length around an object.
The perimeter of this hexagon is 6 inches.

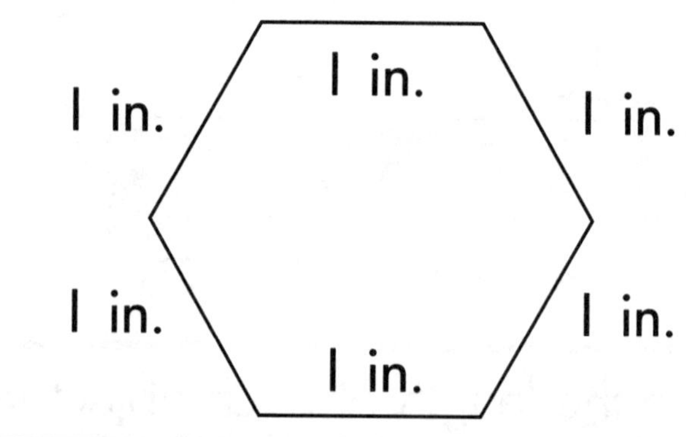

Use an inch ruler to measure length.

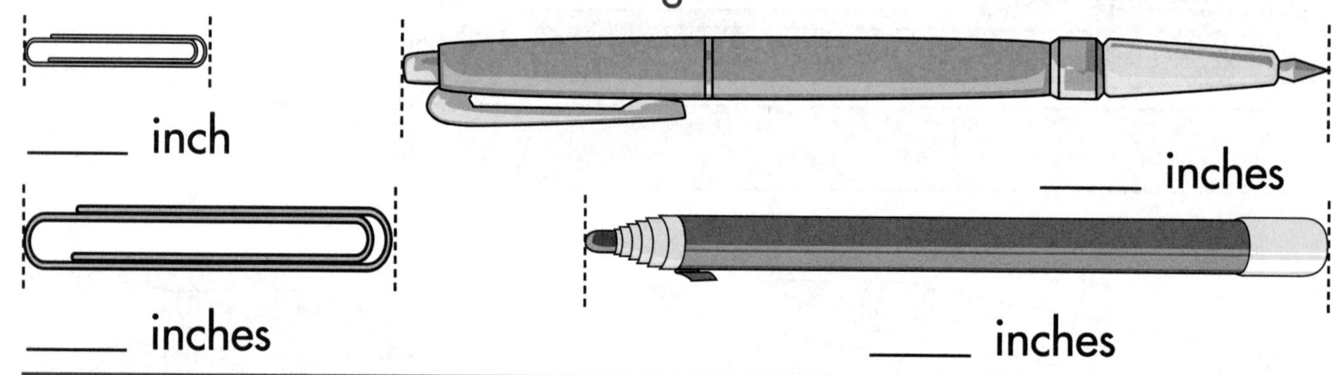

____ inch

____ inches

____ inches

____ inches

Measure the length of each side.
Add the lengths of all sides to get the perimeter.

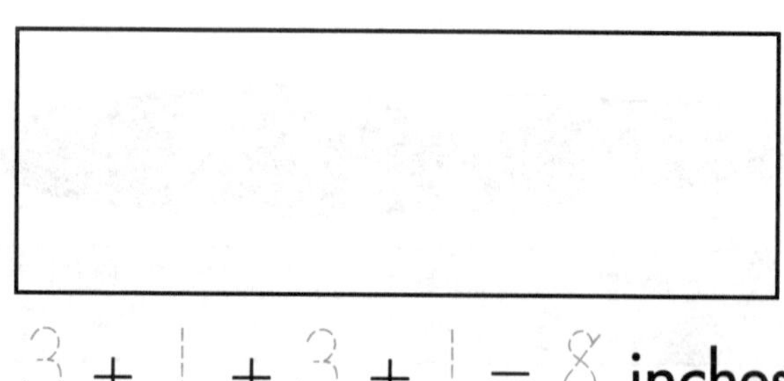

3 + 1 + 3 + 1 = 8 inches

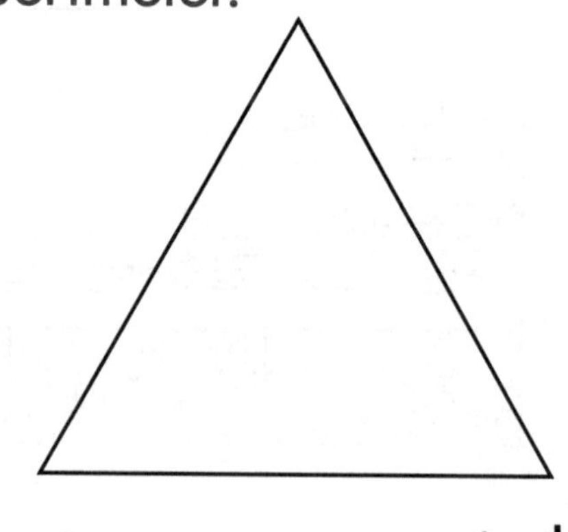

___ + ___ + ___ = ___ inches

___ + ___ + ___ + ___ = ___ inches

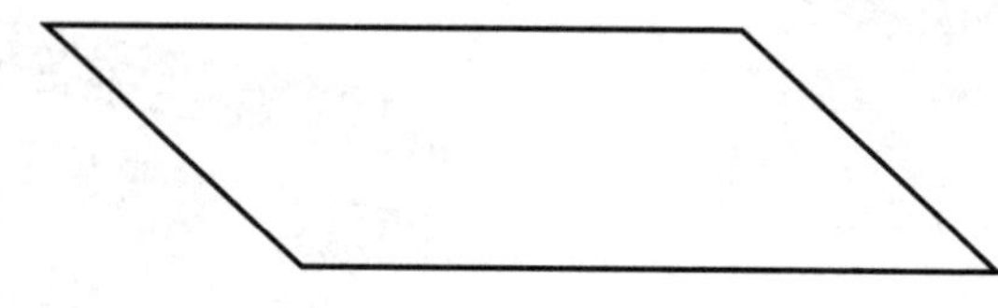

___ + ___ + ___ + ___ = ___ inches

NAME ______________________________

Lesson 7.7 Measuring Length in Centimeters

1 centimeter

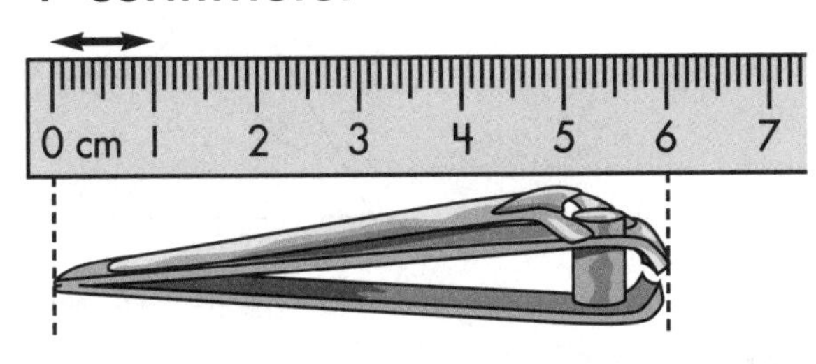

The nail clipper is 6 centimeters long.

Write the length of each object in centimeters.

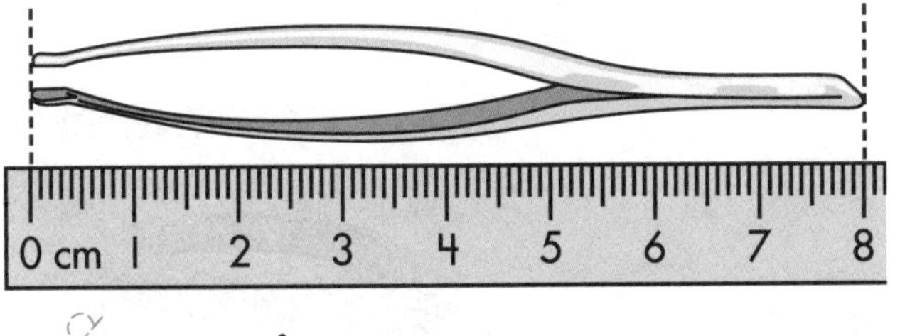

__8__ centimeters

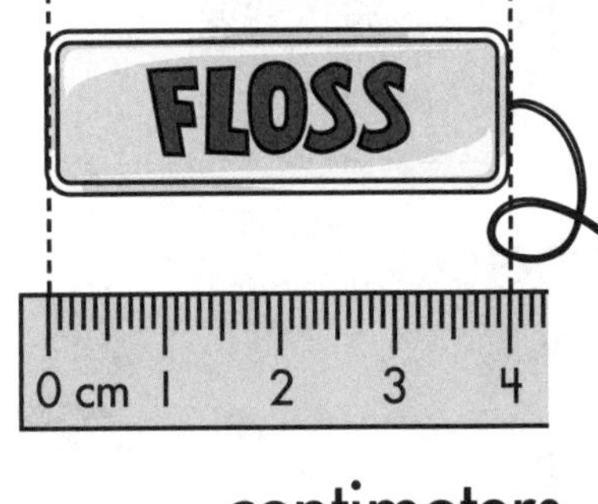

____ centimeters

____ centimeters

____ centimeters

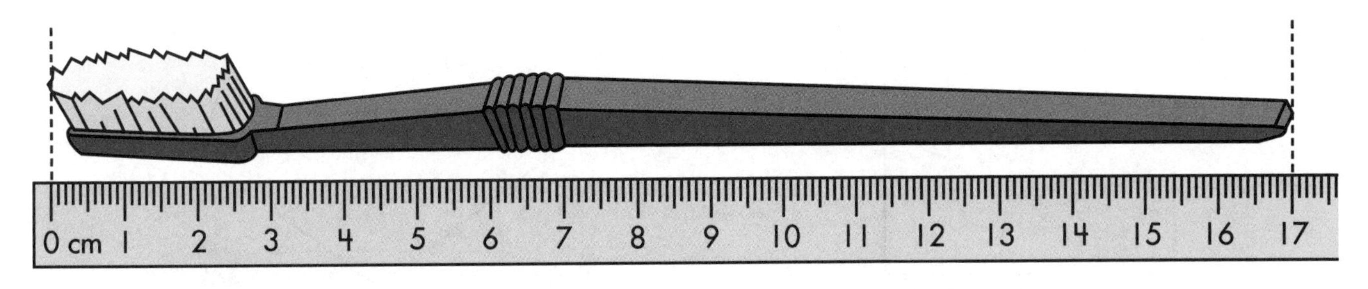

____ centimeters

NAME ____________________

Lesson 7.7 Measuring Length in Centimeters

You can measure perimeter in centimeters.

The perimeter of this triangle is

3 + 3 + 3 = 9 centimeters.

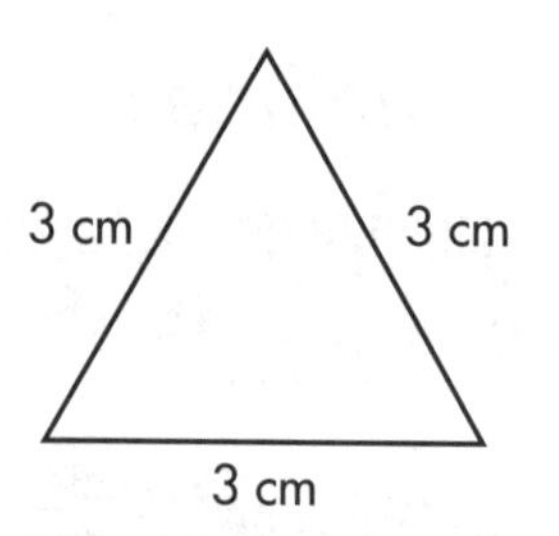

Use a ruler to measure length in centimeters.

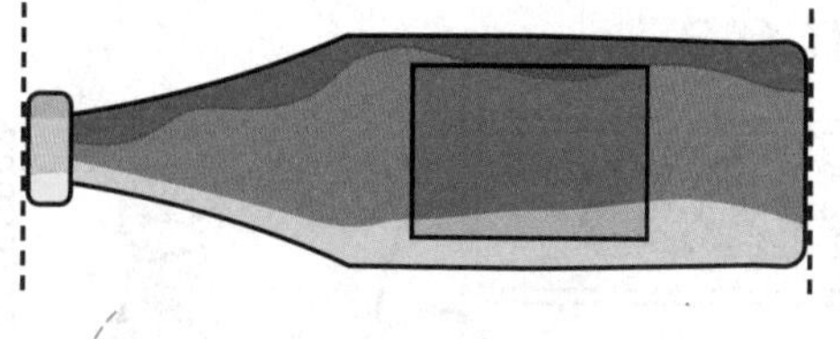

__6__ centimeters

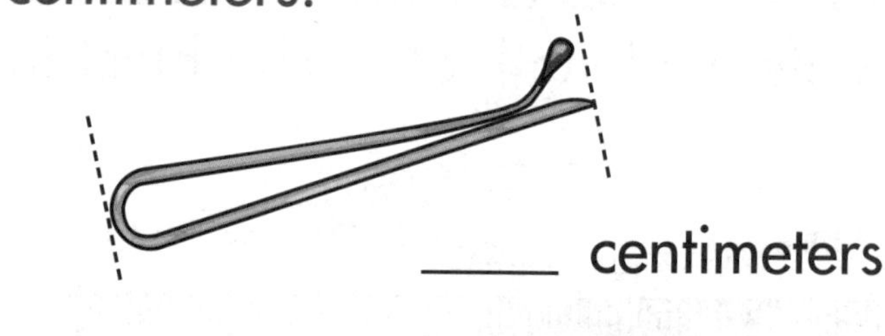

____ centimeters

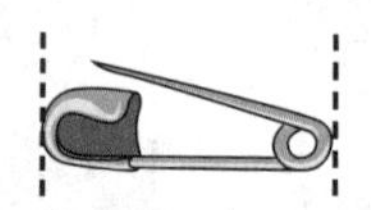

____ centimeters

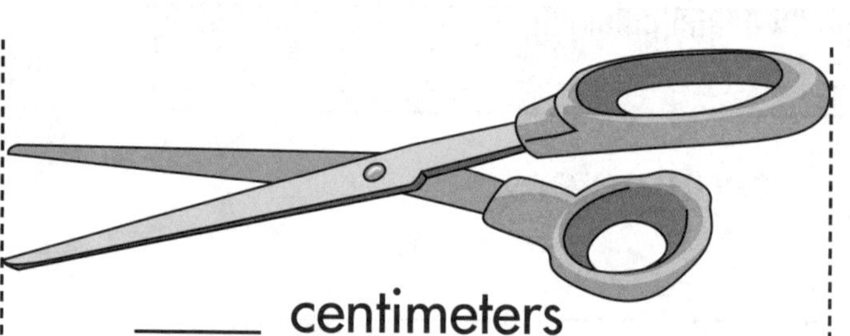

____ centimeters

Measure perimeter. Add the lengths of all sides.

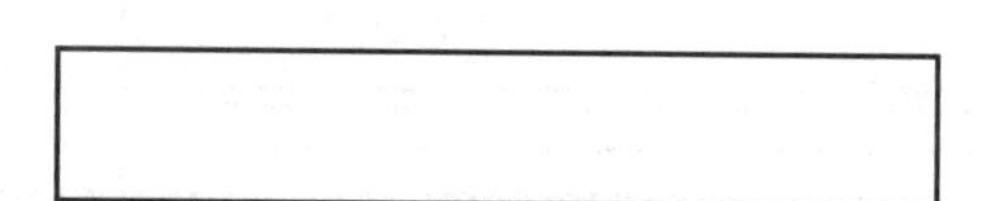

__6__ + __2__ + __6__ + __2__ = __16__ cm

___ + ___ + ___ + ___ = ___ cm

___ + ___ + ___ + ___ = ___ cm

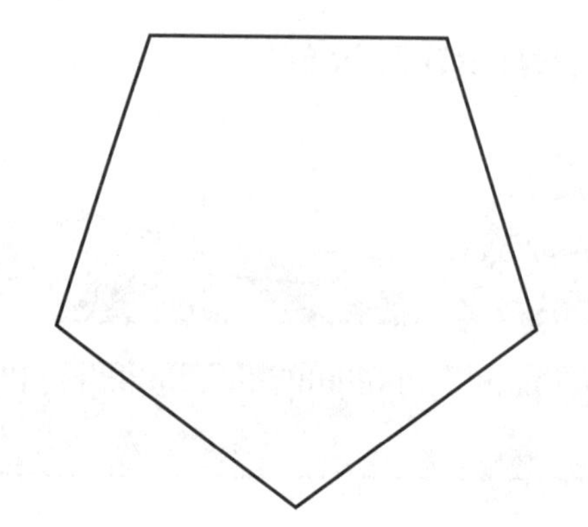

___ + ___ + ___ + ___ + ___ = ___ cm

NAME ____________________

Lesson 7.8 Measuring Area

Area is the number of square units needed to cover a figure.

☐ This is **1 unit**.

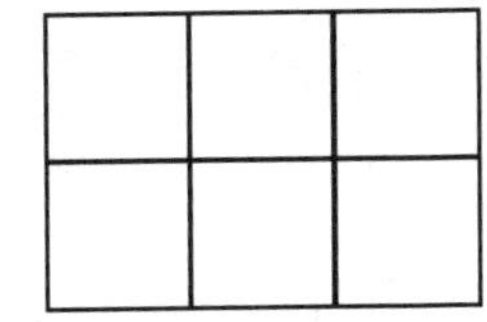

The **area** of this rectangle is 6 units.

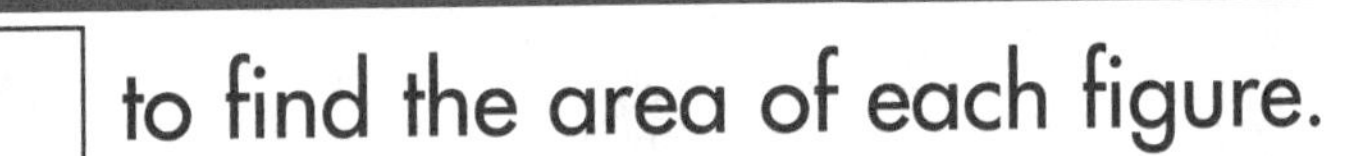

Count the units ☐ to find the area of each figure.

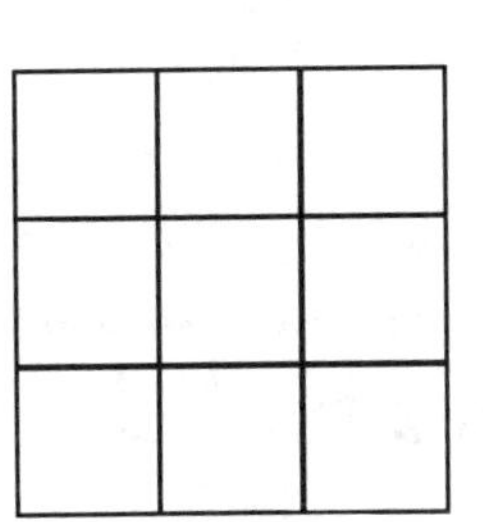

9 square units

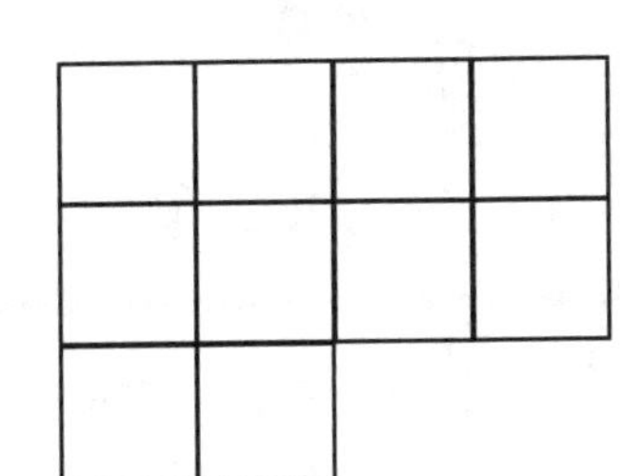

_____ square units

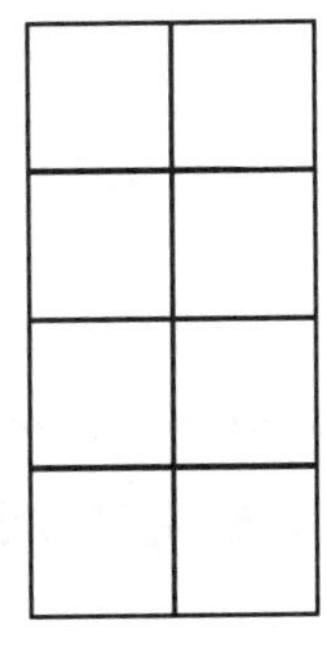

_____ square units

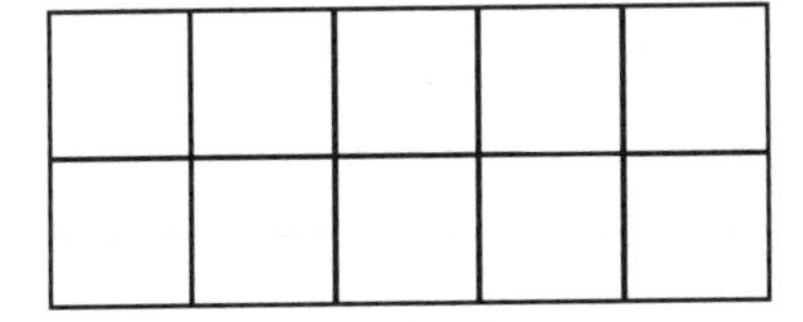

_____ square units

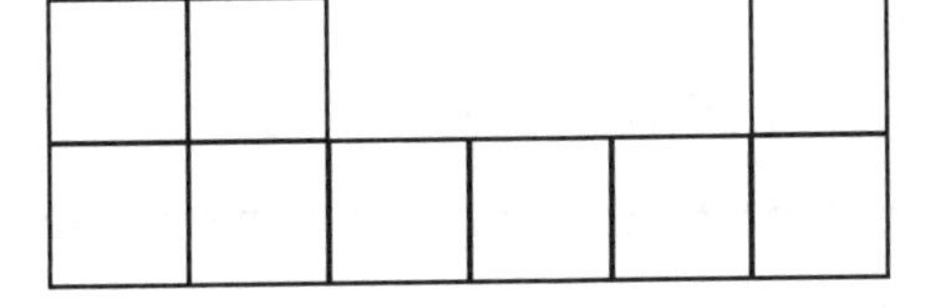

_____ square units

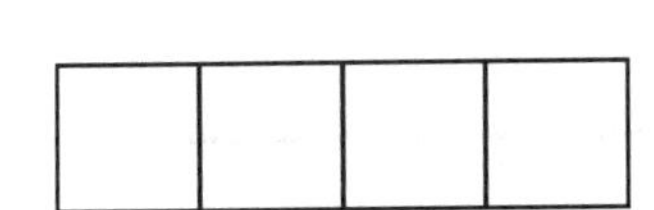

_____ square units

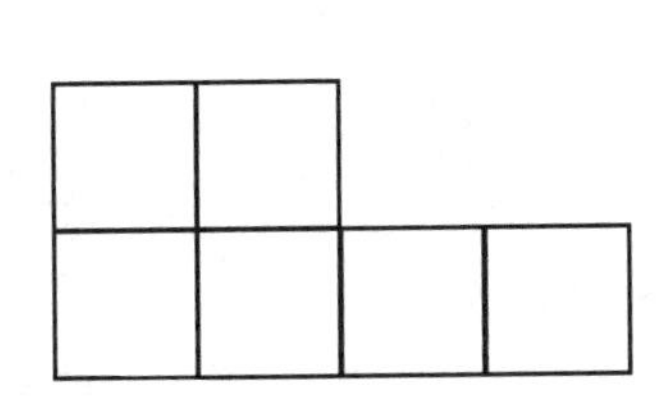

_____ square units

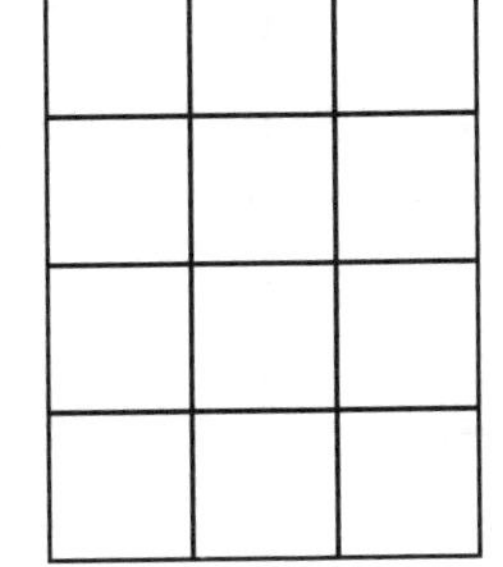

_____ square units

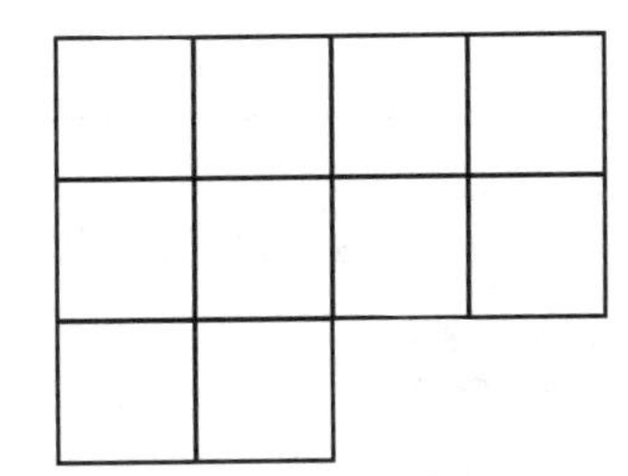

_____ square units

NAME ______________________________

Lesson 7.9 Measuring Liquid Volume

     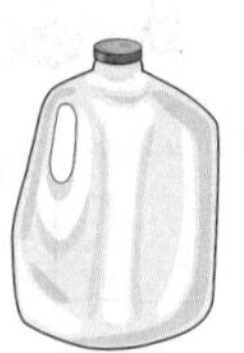

2 cups = 1 pint   2 pints = 1 quart   4 quarts = 1 gallon

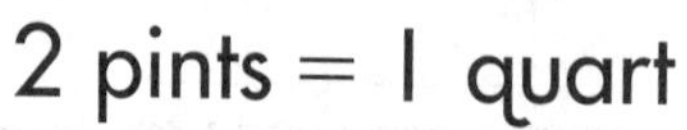

 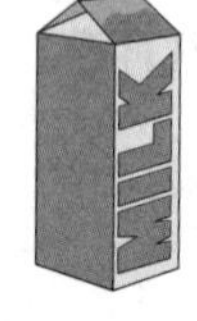  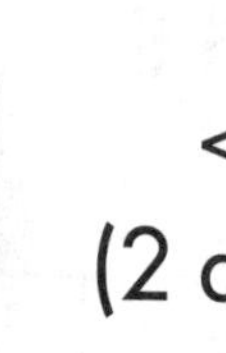  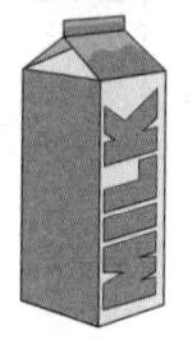 

(1 quart) < (1 liter) < (2 quarts)

1 quart is less than 1 liter. One liter is less than 2 quarts.

Circle the correct words. Use the information above for help.

2 cups — is greater than / is equal to / (is less than) — 1 quart

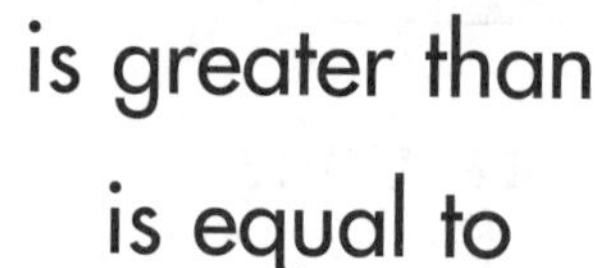 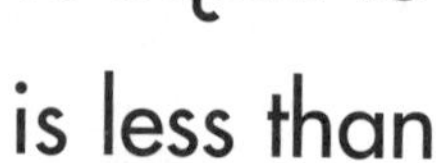 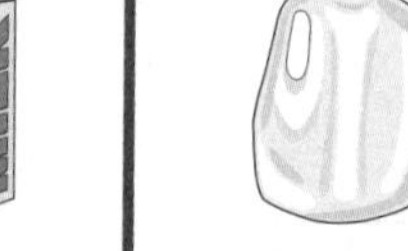 

1 gallon — is greater than / is equal to / is less than — 3 quarts

1 pint — is greater than / is equal to / is less than — 2 cups

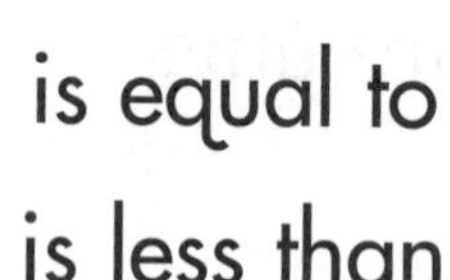 

1 quart — is greater than / is equal to / is less than — 1 liter

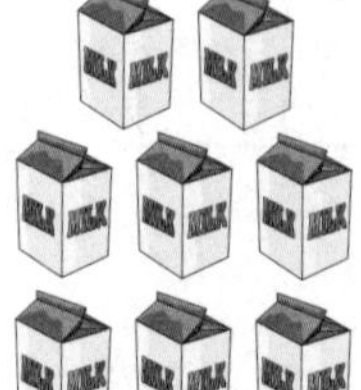 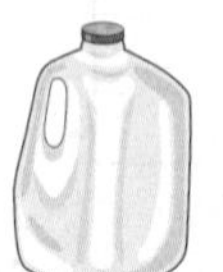

8 pints — is greater than / is equal to / is less than — 1 gallon

1 gallon — is greater than / is equal to / is less than — 4 pints

NAME ______________________

Lesson 7.10 Measuring Temperature

Fahrenheit and Celsius are different ways to measure temperature.

In Fahrenheit, 90°F means a hot day.

In Fahrenheit, 32°F is freezing.

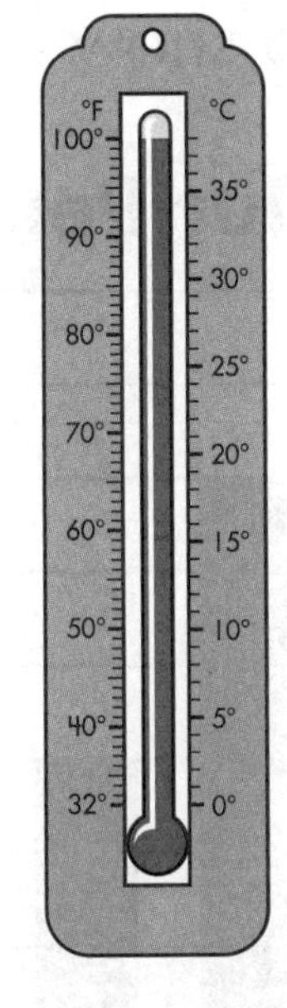

In Celsius, 32°C means a hot day.

In Celsius, 0°C is freezing.

Write the temperature in Fahrenheit and Celsius. Round Fahrenheit to the nearest 10.

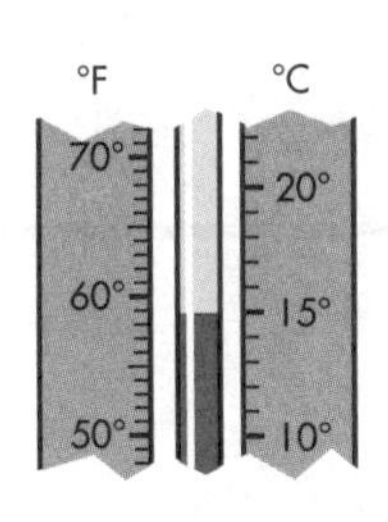

60 °F  15 °C

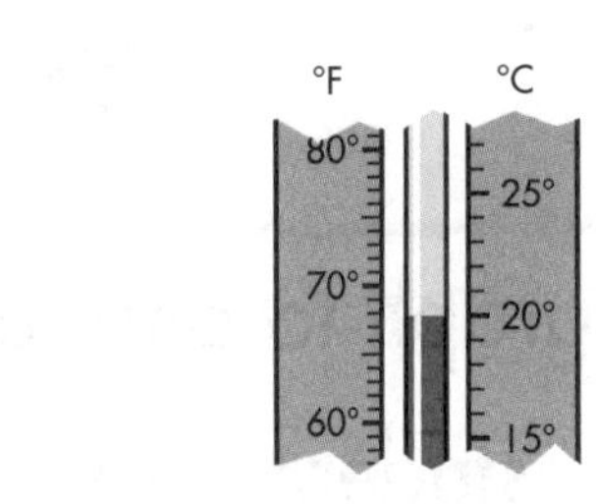

_____ °F  _____ °C

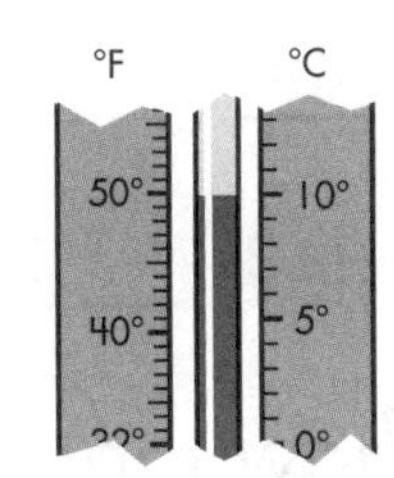

_____ °F  _____ °C

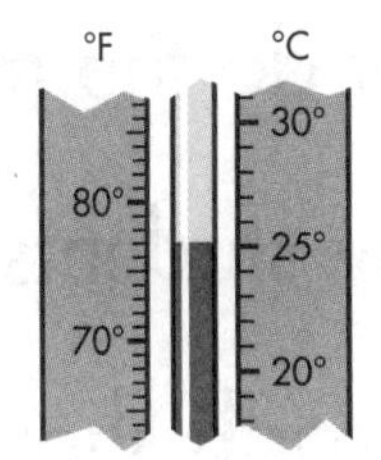

_____ °F _____ °C

NAME ____________________

Lesson 7.11 Reading Picture and Bar Graphs

Keisha asked her classmates about their pets.

She made this bar graph to show the results.

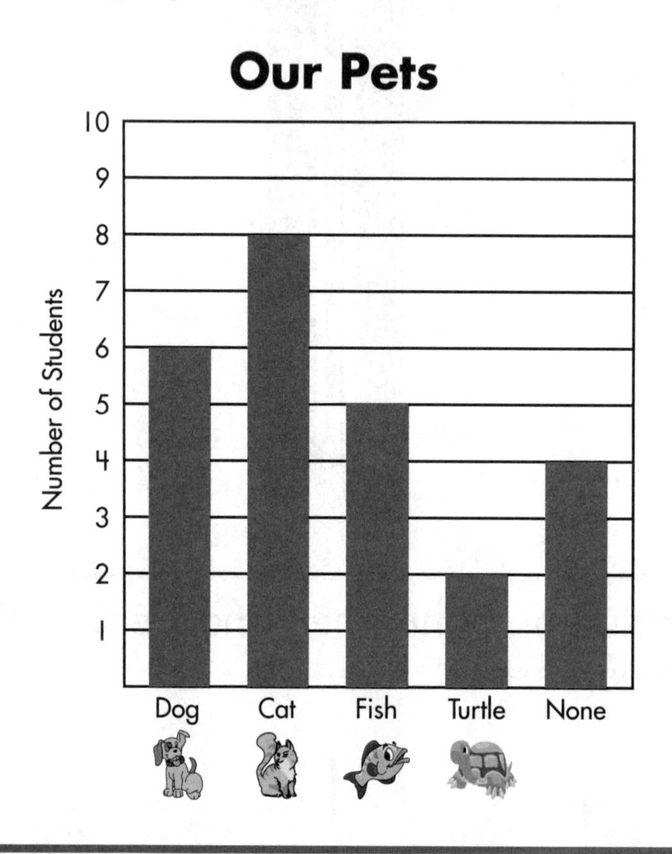

Use the bar graph to answer the questions.

How many students have a dog or a cat? ________

How many students have no pets? ________

Which pet do the most students have? ________

How many students have either a fish or turtle? ________

The bar graph shows that Keisha talked to how many students? ________

Lesson 7.11 Reading Picture and Bar Graphs

Carlos polled his classmates about their favorite fruits.

He made this picture graph with the results. One piece of fruit on the graph means one person.

Our Favorite Fruits

Apples	
Oranges	
Bananas	
Grapes	
Pears	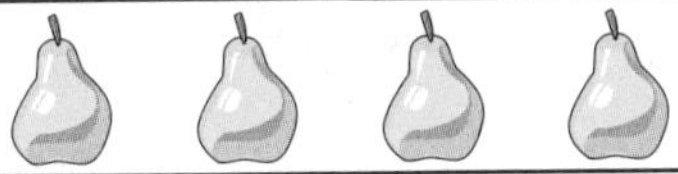

Use the picture graph to answer the questions.

How many classmates chose either bananas or oranges? ________

How many classmates chose grapes or pears? ________

Which fruit did the most classmates choose? ________

How many classmates did *not* choose apples, oranges, or bananas? ________

How many more classmates chose apples than chose grapes? ________

The picture graph shows the favorite fruit of how many students? ________

NAME ____________________

Lesson 7.11 Reading Picture and Bar Graphs

Sam and his friends collect baseball cards. This picture graph shows how many cards they have.

Our Baseball Cards

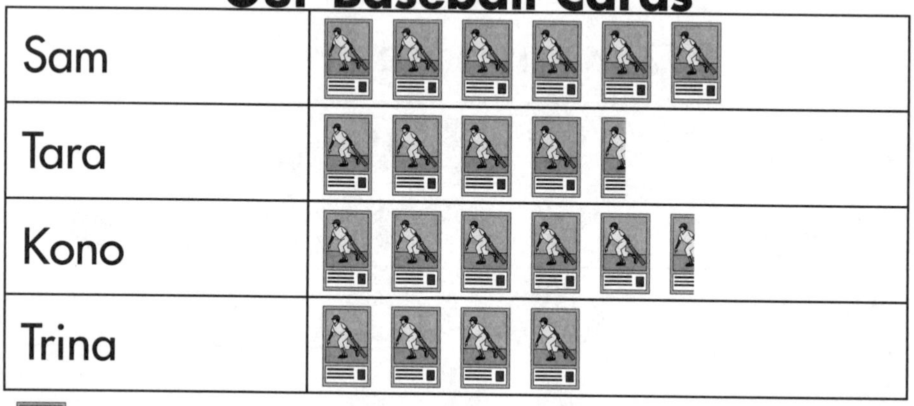

Sam	
Tara	
Kono	
Trina	

= 2 baseball cards

Use the picture graph to answer the questions.

How many cards do the friends have in all? 40

How many cards does Sam have? ________

Who has the fewest cards? ________

How many cards does Kono have? ________

How many cards do Tara and Trina have together? ________

Tara and Trina put their cards together into one collection.

How many more cards do they have together compared to Sam? ________

NAME ____________________

Check What You Learned

Measurement

Use a centimeter ruler. Measure each object.

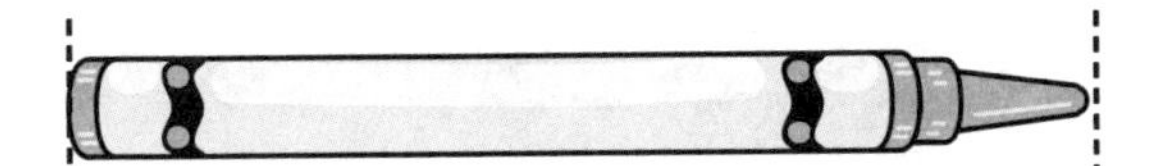

______ centimeters

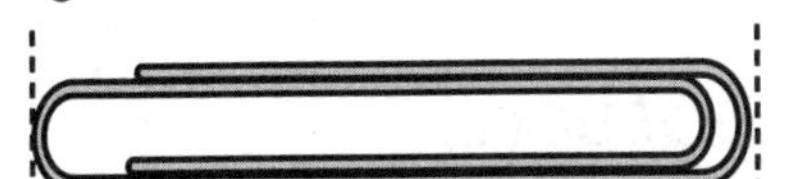

______ centimeters

This is one square unit. 

What is the area of the figure?

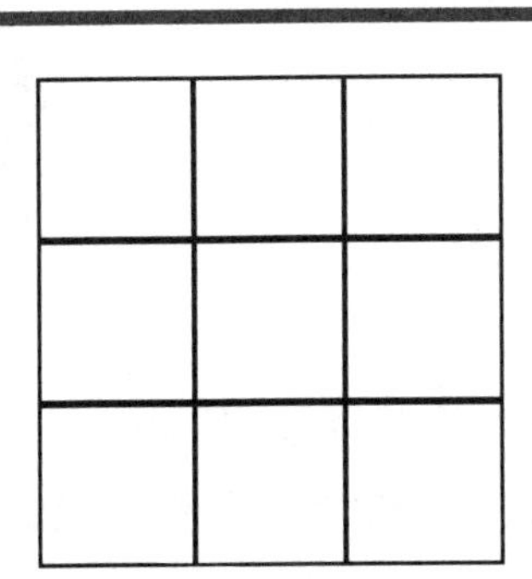

______ square units

Circle the correct words.

4 cups

is greater than

is equal to

is less than

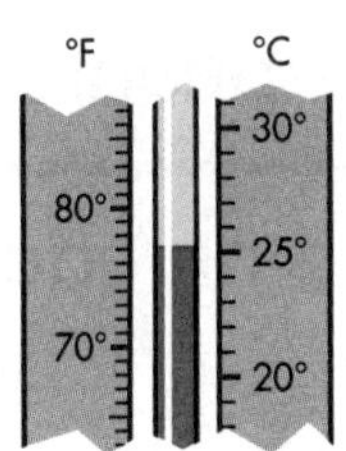

2 quarts

Write the temperature in °F and °C. Round °F to the nearest 10.

______°F ______°C

Use the calendar to answer the questions.

How many days are in the month? ______

What day of the week is May 17?

____

May						
S	M	T	W	Th	F	Sa
1	2	3	4	5	6	7
8	9	10	11	12	13	14
15	16	17	18	19	20	21
22	23	24	25	26	27	28
29	30	31				

NAME ____________________

Check What You Learned

Measurement

Favorite Sports

Baseball	
Football	
Basketball	
Soccer	

Use the picture graph to answer the questions. Each picture means one person chose the sport.

Which sport did most people choose? ________

Which sport did 7 people choose? ________

How many people chose football or basketball? ______

Read the time on each clock. Write the time on the line below.

____ : ____   ____ o'clock   ____ : ____

Add the two money amounts.

¢
+ ¢
¢

¢
+ ¢
¢

Check What You Know

Geometry

Circle the shape named.

rectangular solid 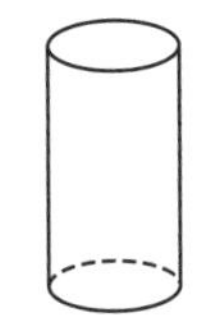 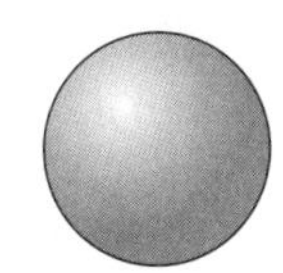 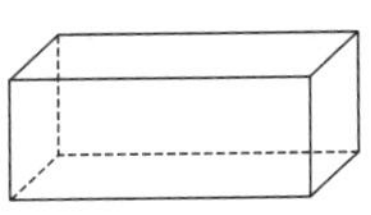 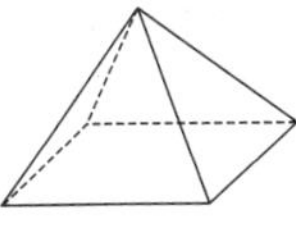

square pyramid 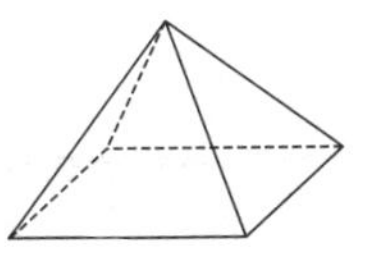 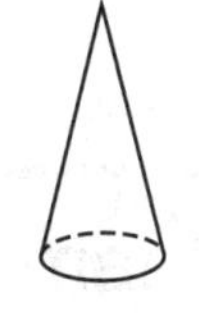 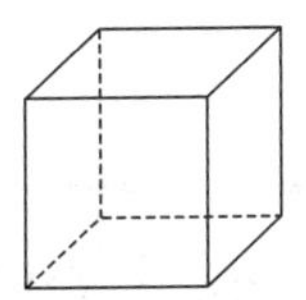 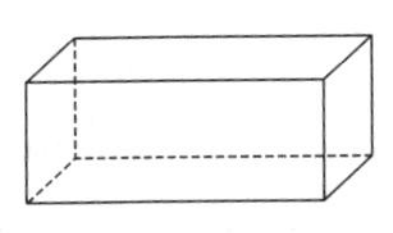

sphere  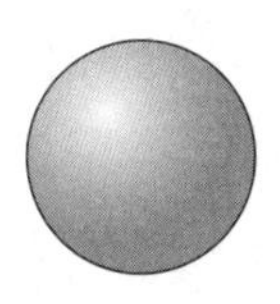 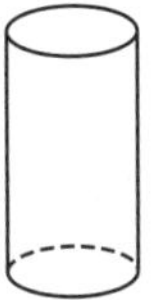 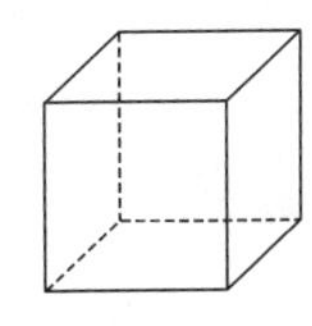

Name each shape.

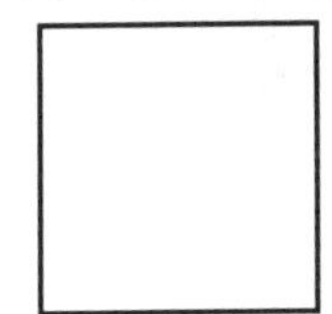 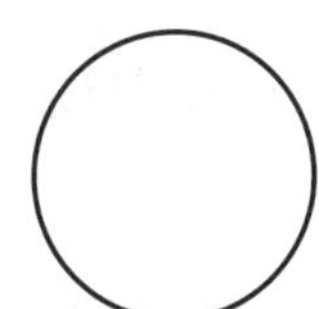 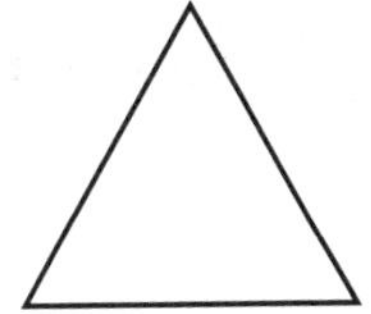 

__________ __________ __________ __________

Draw a line of symmetry if the shape is symmetrical.

NAME ______________________

Check What You Know

Geometry

Draw the solid shapes. Color them.

rectangular solid

cone

Draw the plane shapes. Color them.

triangle

square

Circle the plane shapes that are faces on the solid shape.

rectangular solid

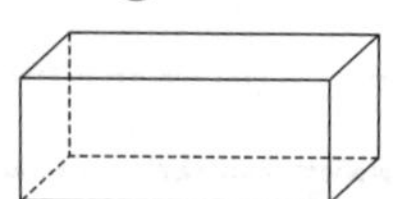

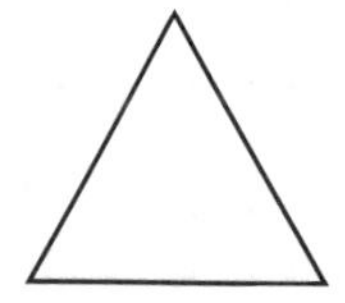 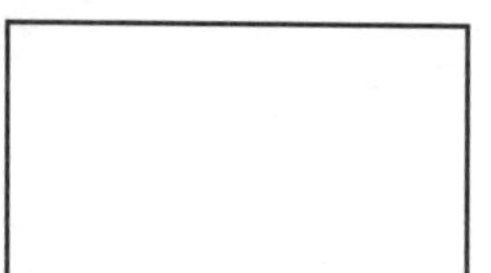 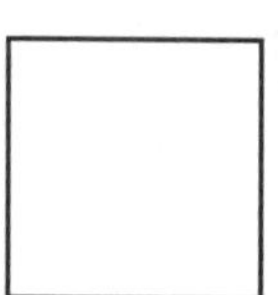

square pyramid

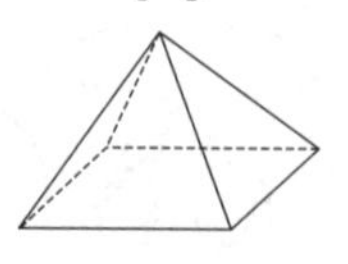

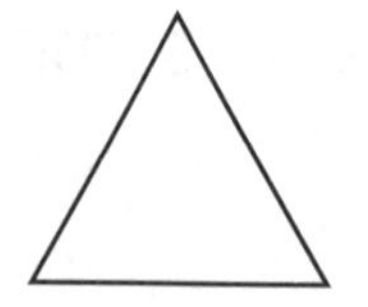 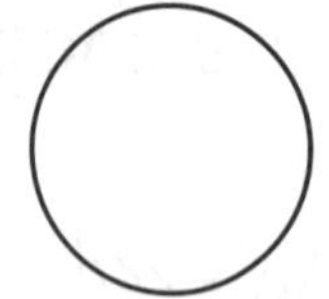 

cylinder

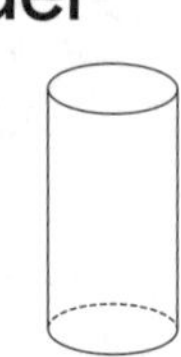

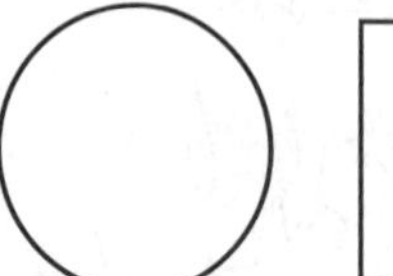  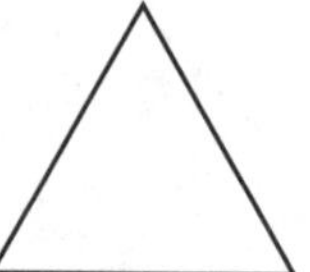

NAME ____________________

Lesson 8.1 Plane Shapes

square

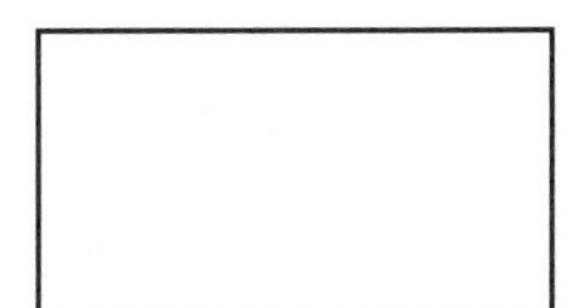
rectangle

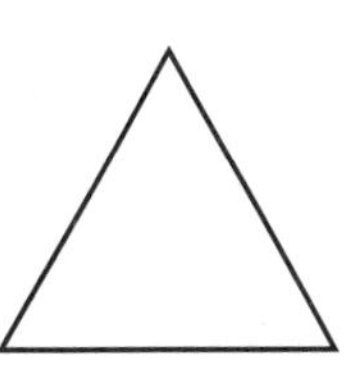
triangle

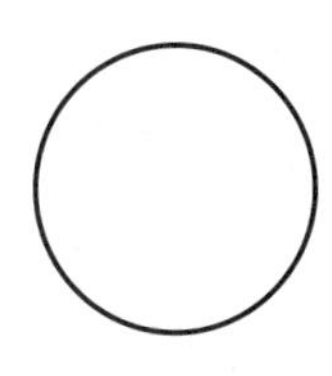
circle

Name each shape.

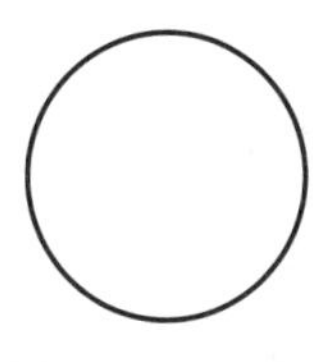
circle

rectangle

____

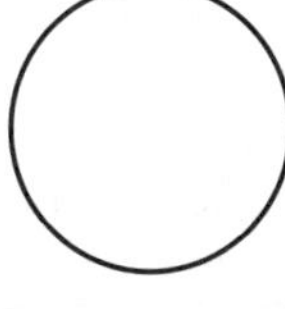
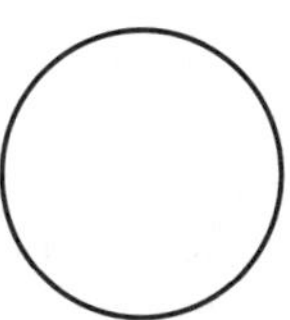
____

____

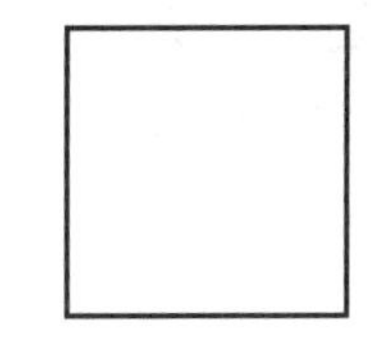
____

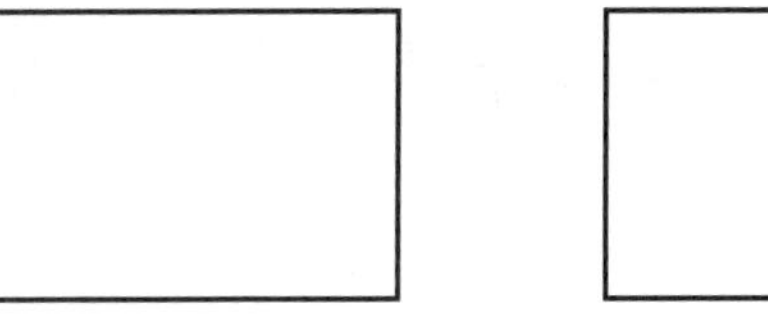
____

____

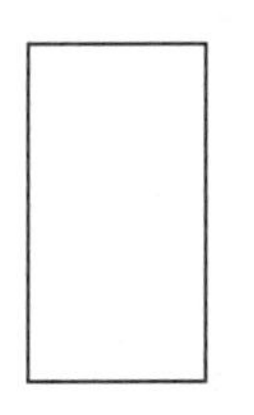
____

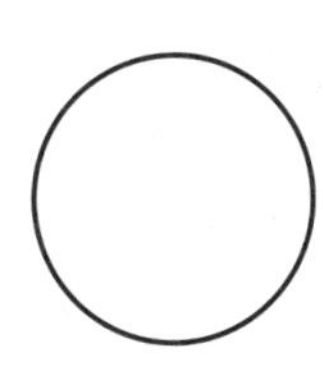
____

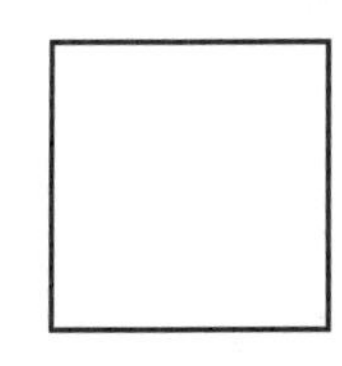
____

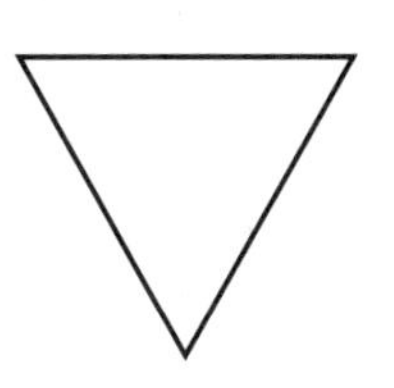
____

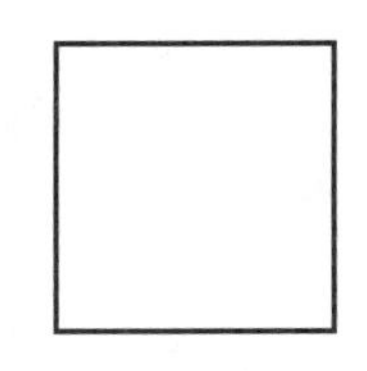
____

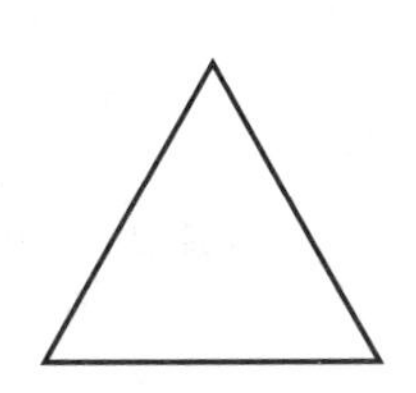
____

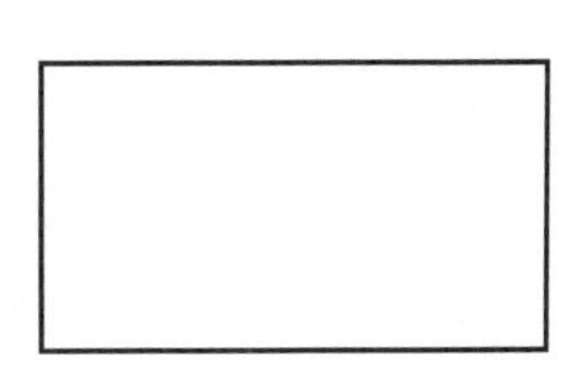
____

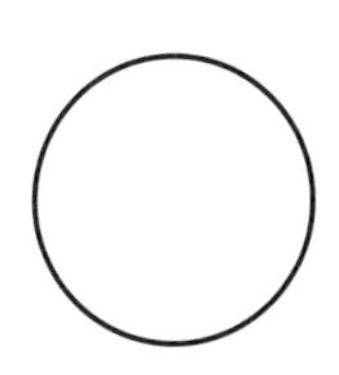
____

NAME ______________________

Lesson 8.2 Solid Shapes

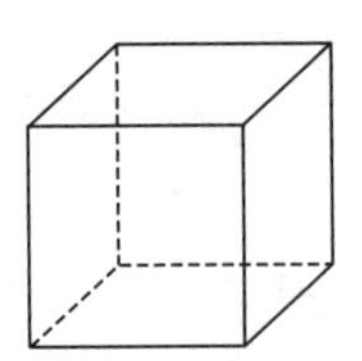

cube

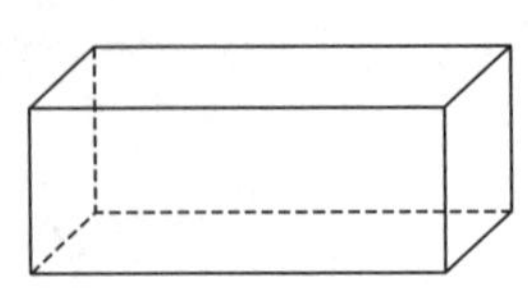

rectangular solid

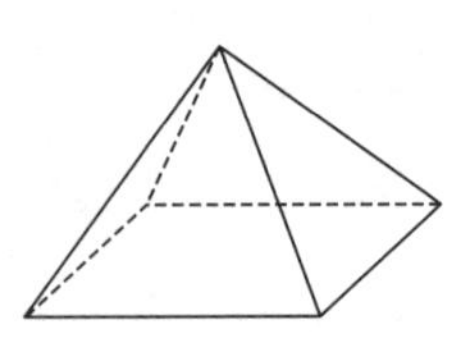

square pyramid

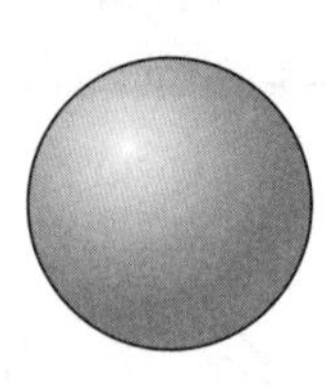

sphere

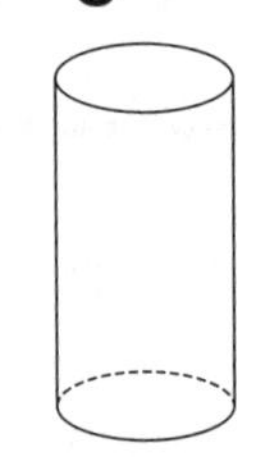

cylinder

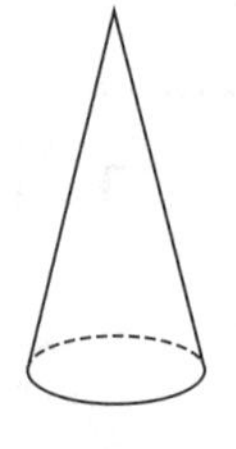

cone

Circle the shape.

rectangular solid 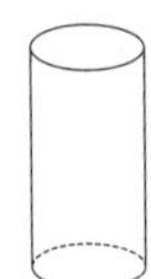 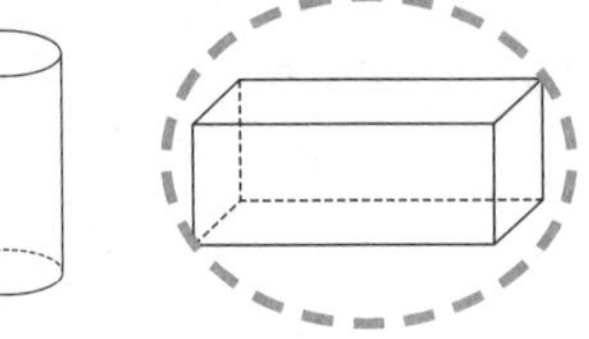 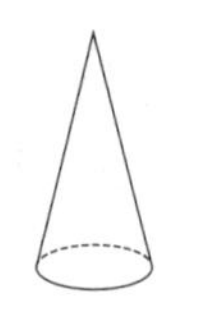 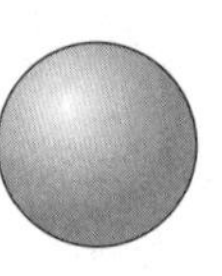

cylinder   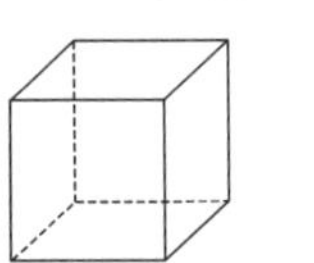 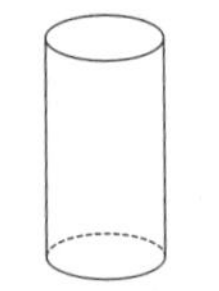

square pyramid 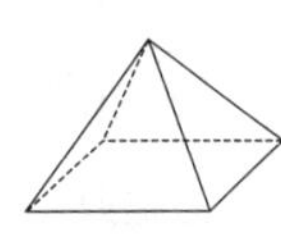 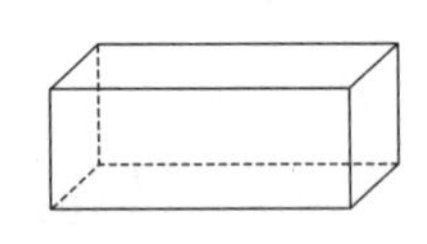  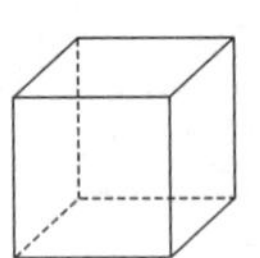

sphere 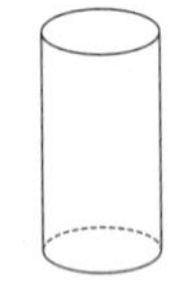 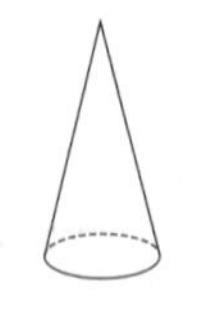  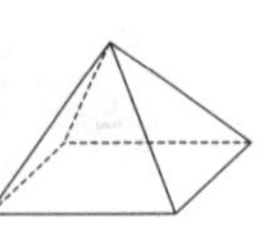

cube 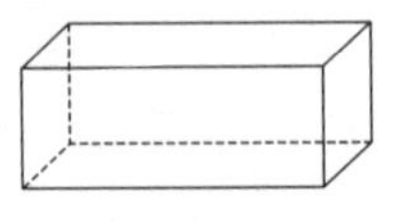 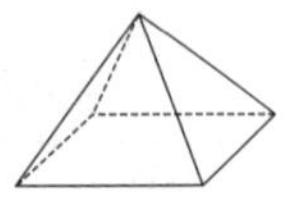 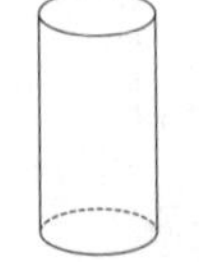 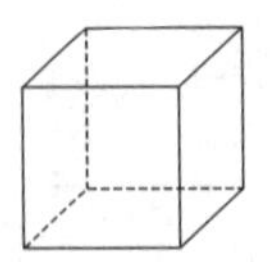

cone  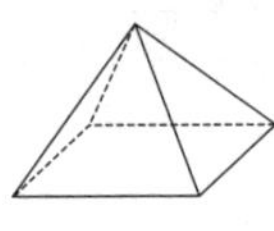 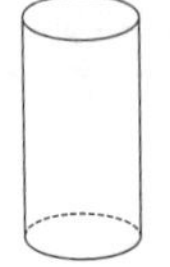 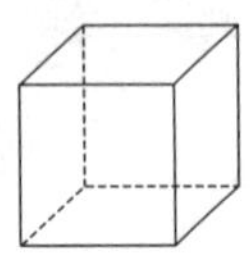

NAME ____________________

Lesson 8.3 Comparing Shapes

A **face** is a flat surface of a solid.

An **edge** is where 2 sides meet.

A **corner** is where 3 or more sides meet.

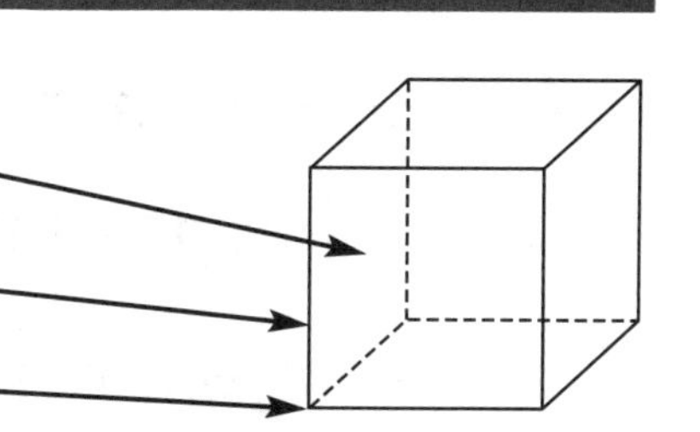

Solid figures are in the left column. Circle the shape or shapes on the right that are faces of each solid.

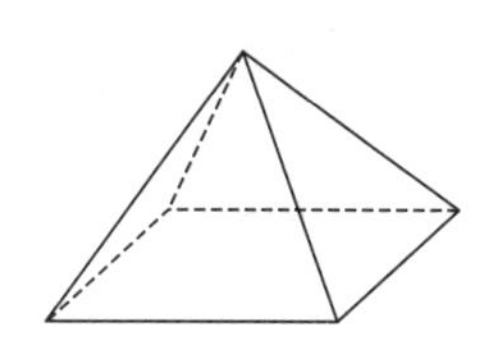 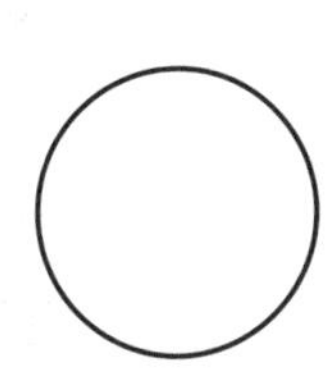 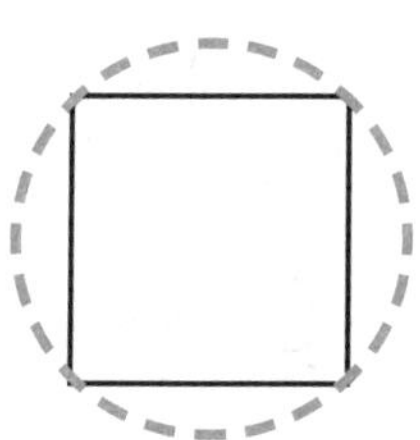 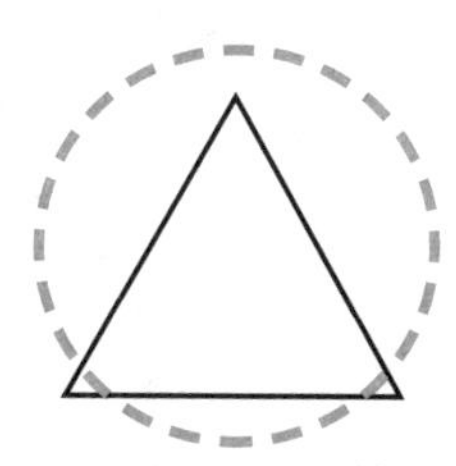

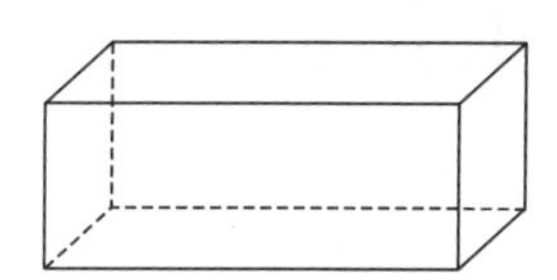  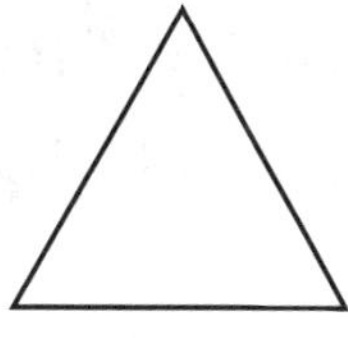 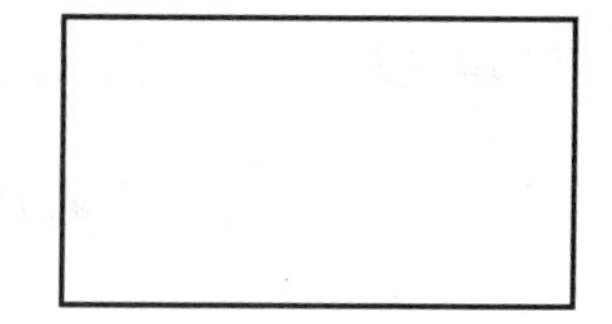

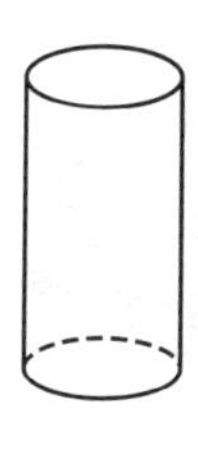  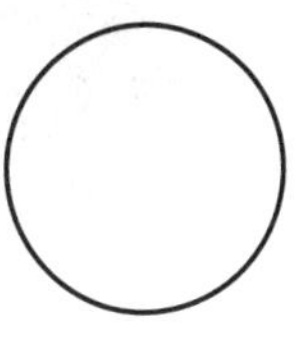 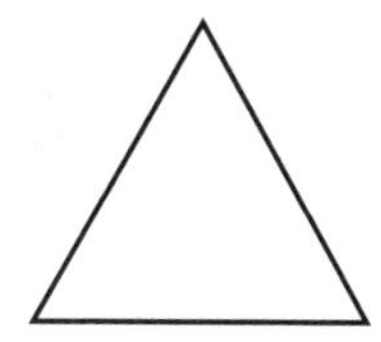

 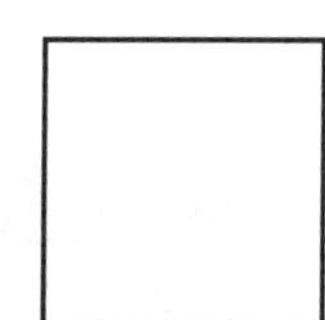 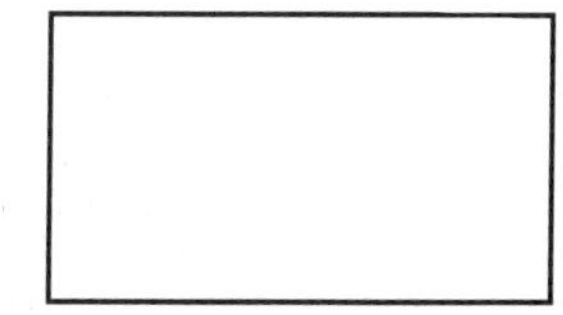 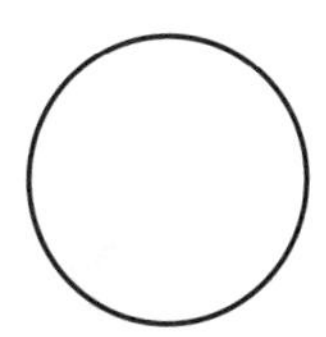

Look at the sphere. Answer the questions.

Does the sphere have any faces? no

Does it have any edges? ________

Does it have any corners? ________

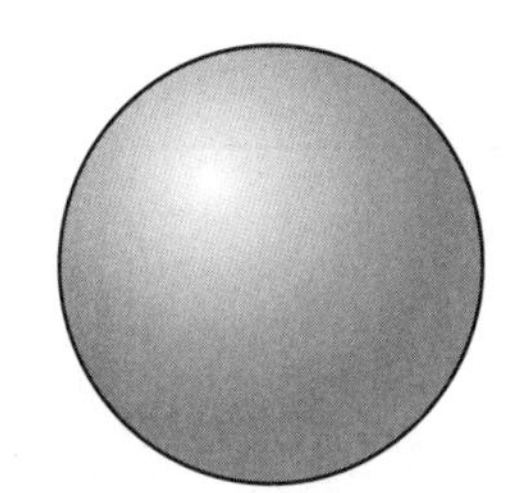

NAME ______________________

Lesson 8.4 Symmetry

A figure or shape is **symmetrical** when one-half of it is the mirror image of the other half.

These objects are symmetrical. They have a line symmetry.

These objects are **asymmetrical**. They have no line of symmetry.

Draw a line of symmetry through each symmetrical shape.
Circle each asymmetrical shape.

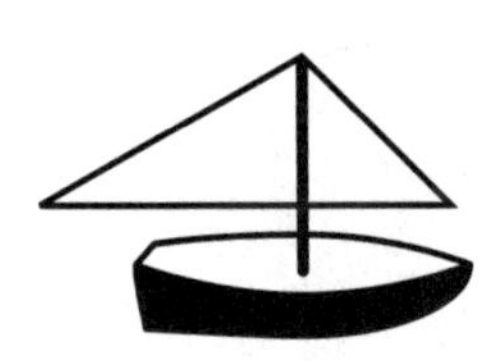

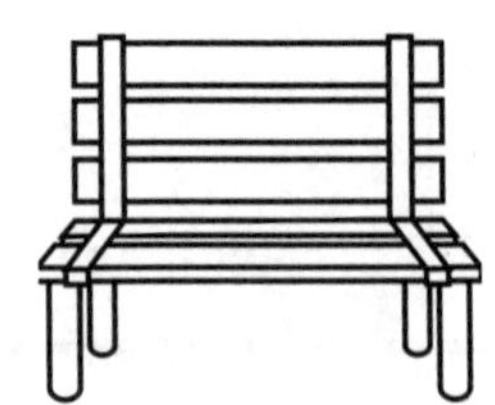

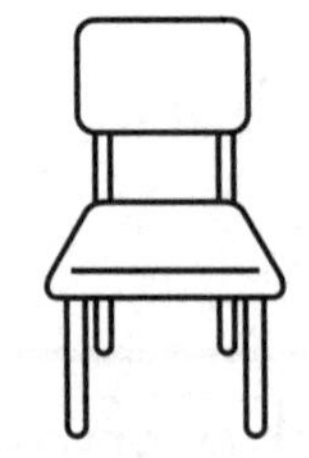

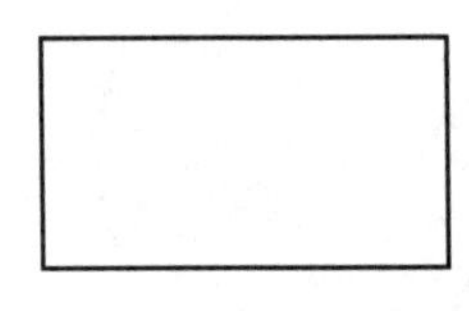

NAME ____________________

Lesson 8.5 Drawing Shapes

Draw plane shapes.

Look at the shape.	Draw your own shape. Color it.
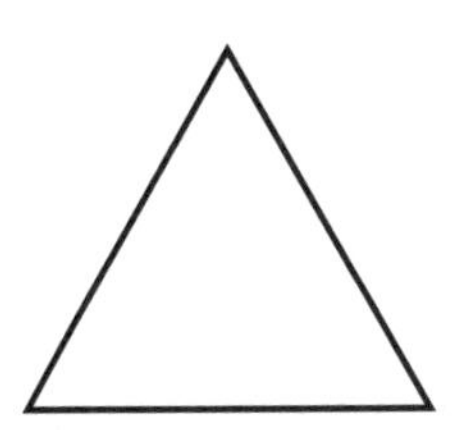 A triangle has 3 sides.	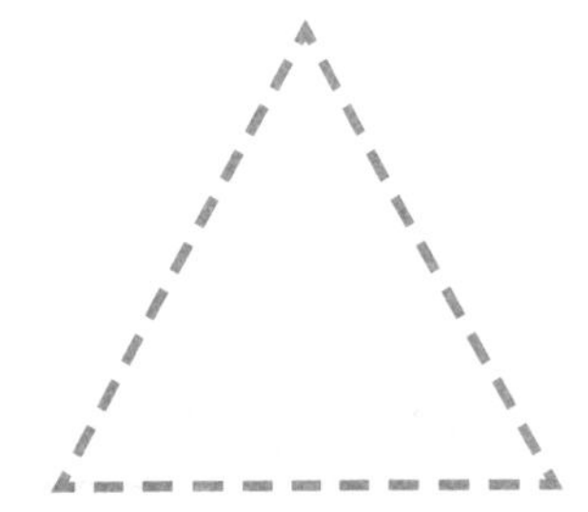
A square has 4 equal sides.	
 A rectangle has 2 pairs of equal sides.	
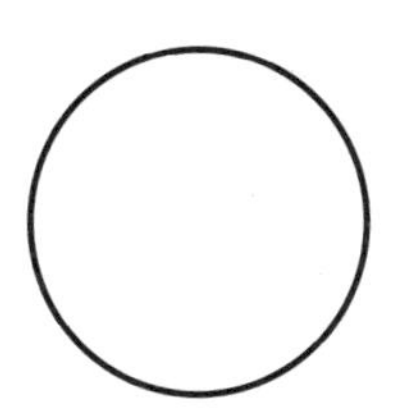 A circle is totally round.	

NAME ____________________

Lesson 8.5 Drawing Shapes

Draw solid shapes.

Look at the shape.	Draw your own shape. Color it.
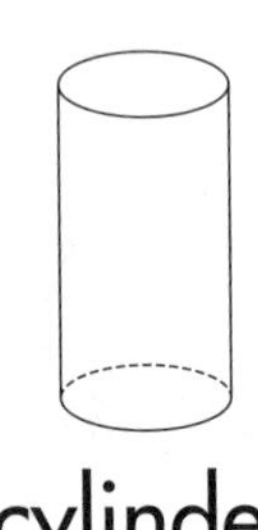 cylinder	
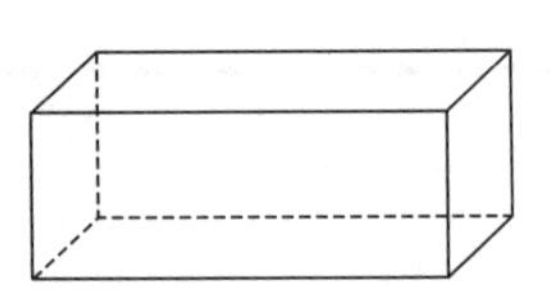 rectangular solid	
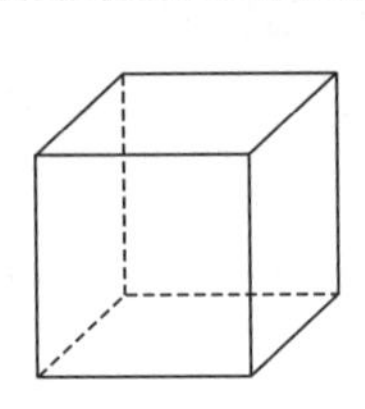 cube	
 cone	
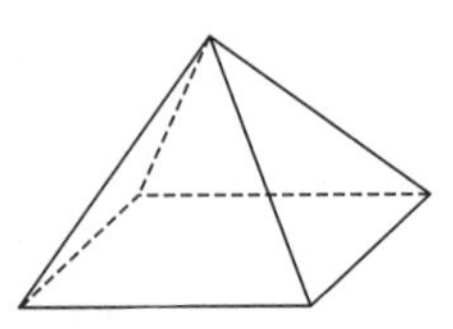 square pyramid	

NAME ______________________

Check What You Learned

Geometry

Name each shape.

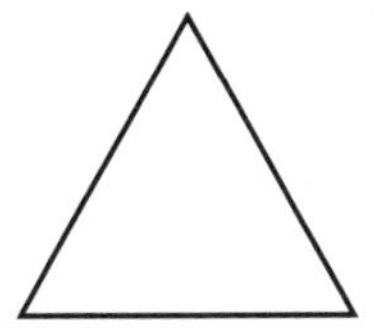 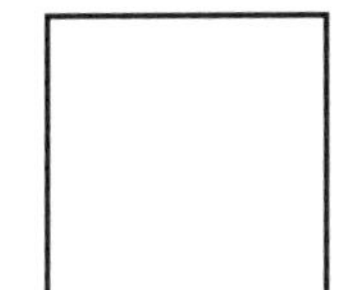  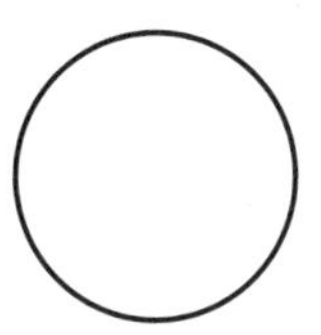

__________ __________ __________ __________

Draw a line of symmetry if the shape is symmetrical.
Circle the shape if it is asymmetrical.

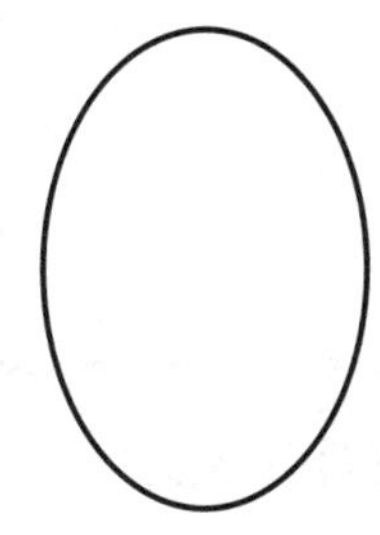  

Circle the shape named.

cylinder 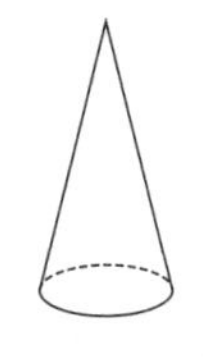 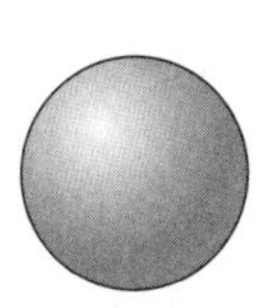 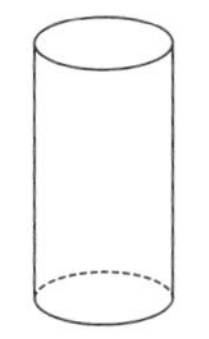 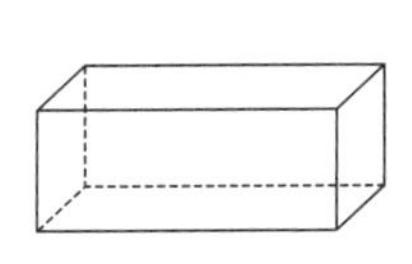

cube 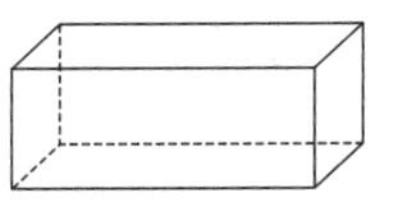 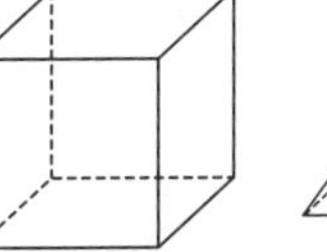 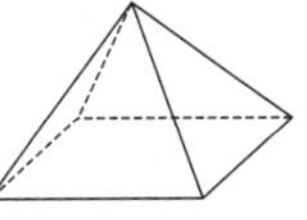 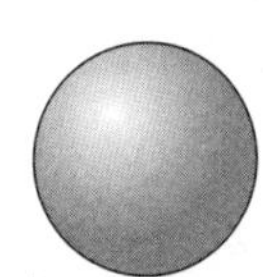

cone 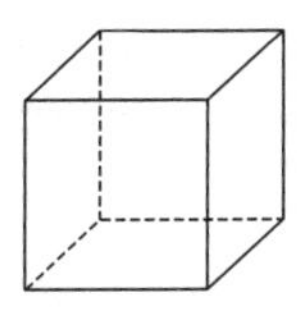 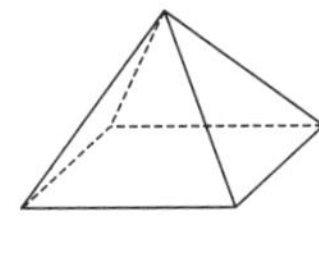 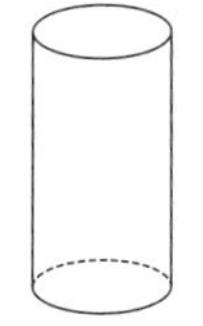 

CHAPTER 8 POSTTEST

NAME ______________________

Check What You Learned

Geometry

Draw the plane shapes. Color them.

circle

rectangle

Draw the solid shapes. Color them.

cylinder

cube

Circle the plane shapes that are faces on the solid shape.

cube 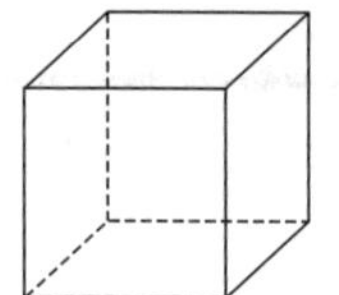 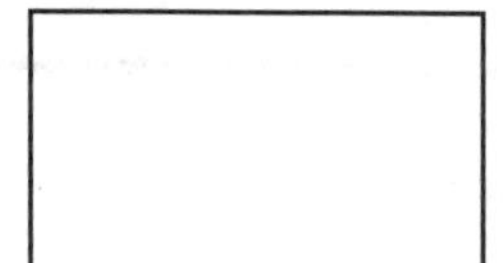  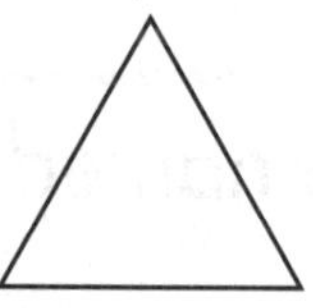

cone   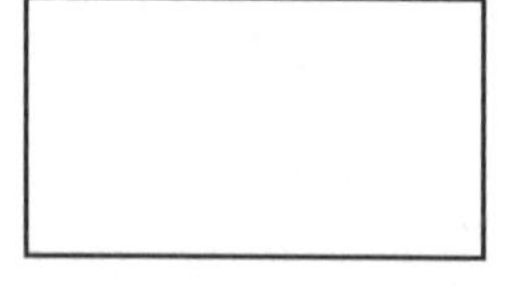 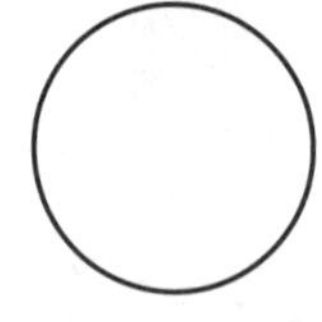

square pyramid 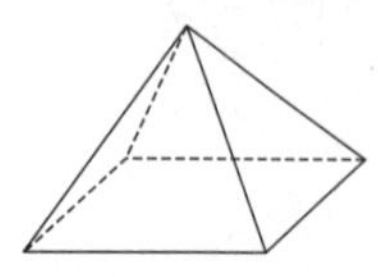  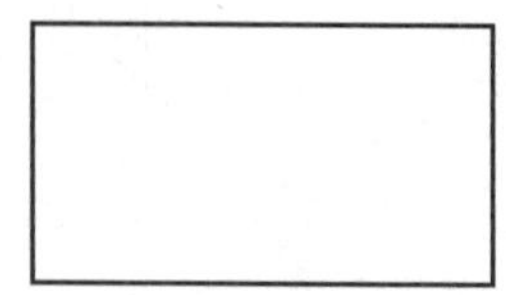 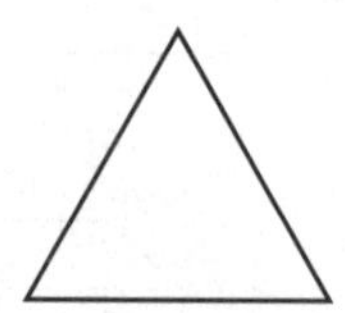

NAME ______________________

Check What You Know

Preparing for Algebra

Draw the next shape in the pattern.

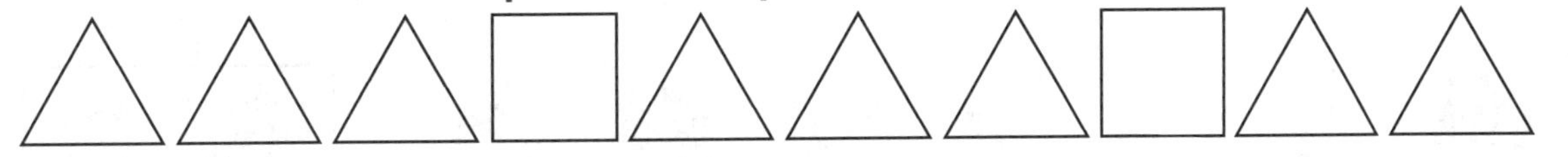
______

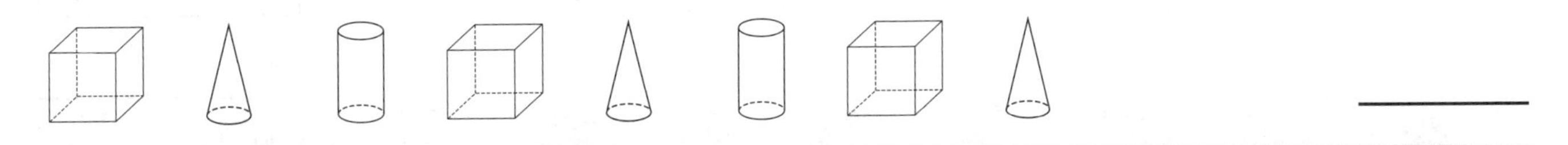
______

Draw the next two shapes in the pattern.

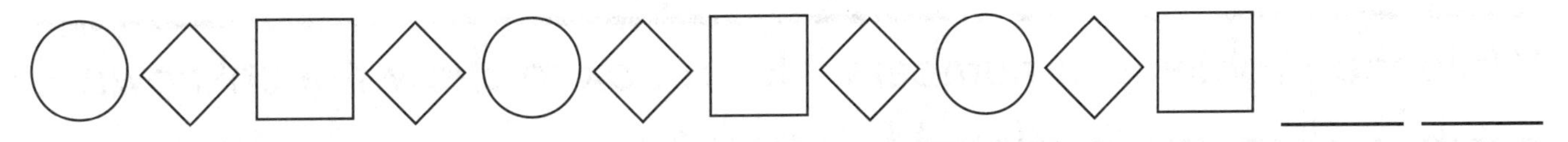
______ ______

Use subtraction to find the number pattern.
Write the number that comes next.

1 5 9 13 17 ______

+____ +____ +____ +____ +____

1 3 7 13 21 ______

+____ +____ +____ +____ +____

Make a related fact to solve. Circle the number that goes in the box.

$11 - \square = 2$ $\square + 4 = 6$ $\square - 4 = 8$ $15 - \square = 6$

______ ______ ______ ______

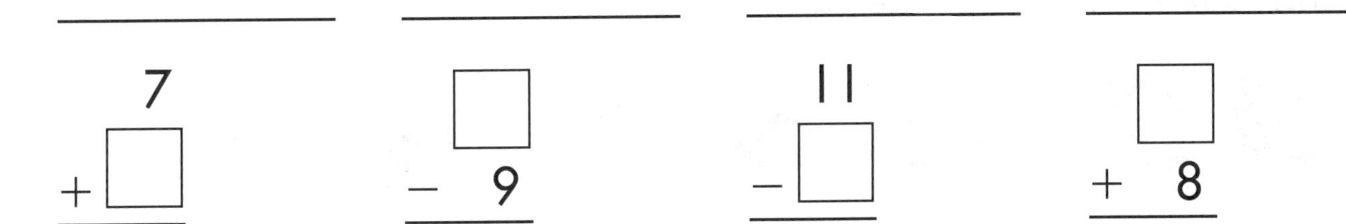

$7 + \square = 10$ $\square - 9 = 9$ $11 - \square = 6$ $\square + 8 = 14$

NAME ____________________

Check What You Know

Preparing for Algebra

Circle the object in the box that should be next in the pattern.

        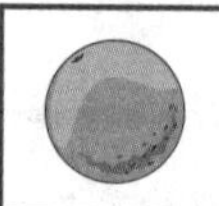 

Write the problems in numbers. Use a box to show the unknown number. Then, use a related fact to solve.

Holly has 9 apples. Her mom buys some more.

Now she has 13 apples. How many apples did her mom buy?

__________ __________ ☐ = ______

Mario has 17 comic books. He lends some to Frank.

Now he has 9. How many comic books did Mario lend to Frank?

__________ __________ ☐ = ______

Write the number of each object in the pattern. Circle the object in the box that should be next.

      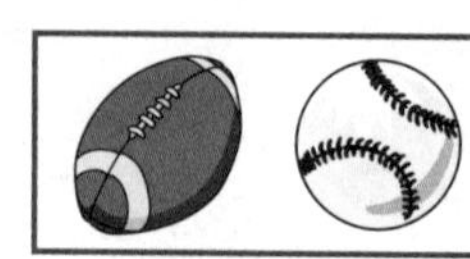

____

NAME ____________________

Lesson 9.1 Patterns

What object should come next in the pattern? Circle it in the box.

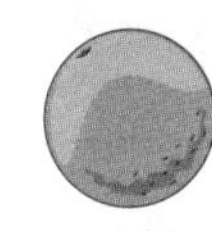
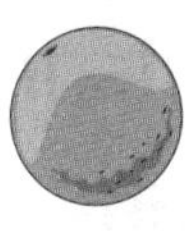

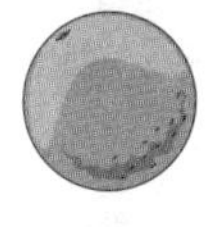

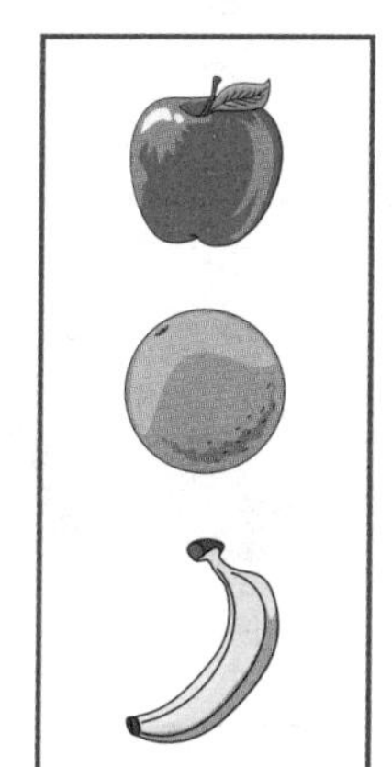

NAME ______________________

Lesson 9.2 Transferring Patterns

Write the numbers shown in the pattern. Circle what comes next.

1, 3, 1, 3

Write the number of each object shown in the pattern. Circle what comes next.

____

____

____

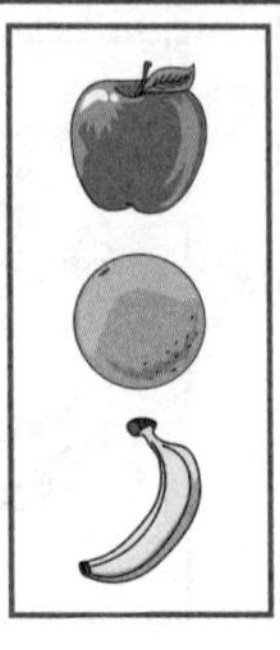

____

NAME ____________________

Lesson 9.3 Number Patterns

What is the number pattern? What is the next number in the pattern?

1 3 6 10 15 21 28 ____

Use subtraction to solve.

1 3 6 10 15 21 28 36

+2 +3 +4 +5 +6 +7 +8

3 − 1 = 2, 6 − 3 = 3, 10 − 6 = 4, 15 − 10 = 5,

21 − 15 = 6, 28 − 21 = 7. Add 8 to find the next number (36).

Use subtraction to find the number pattern. Write the number that comes next.

2 5 8 11 14 17 ____

+____ +____ +____ +____ +____ +____

0 2 6 12 20 30 ____

+____ +____ +____ +____ +____ +____

3 8 13 18 23 28 ____

+____ +____ +____ +____ +____ +____

1 2 5 10 17 26 ____

+____ +____ +____ +____ +____ +____

NAME ______________________

Lesson 9.4 Geometric Patterns

What comes next in the pattern?
Draw the shape.

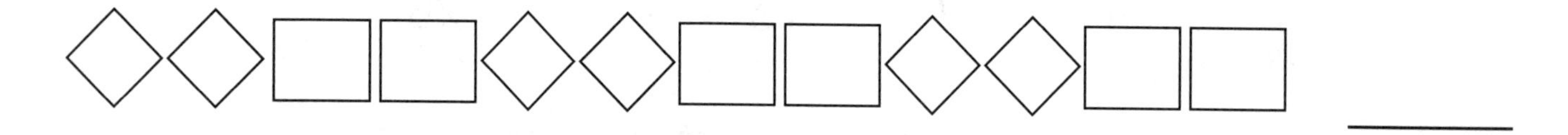

Draw the next two shapes in the pattern.

NAME ____________________

Lesson 9.4 Geometric Patterns

Complete each pattern.

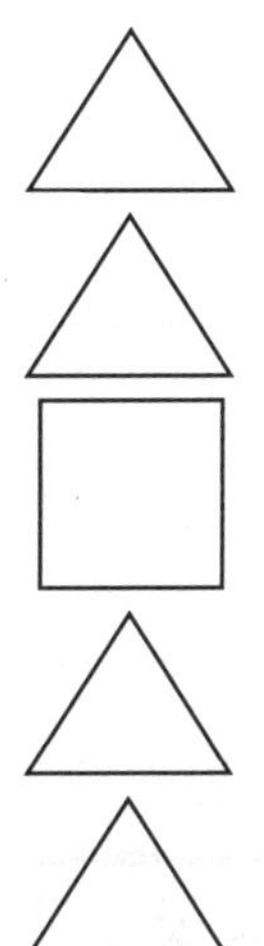
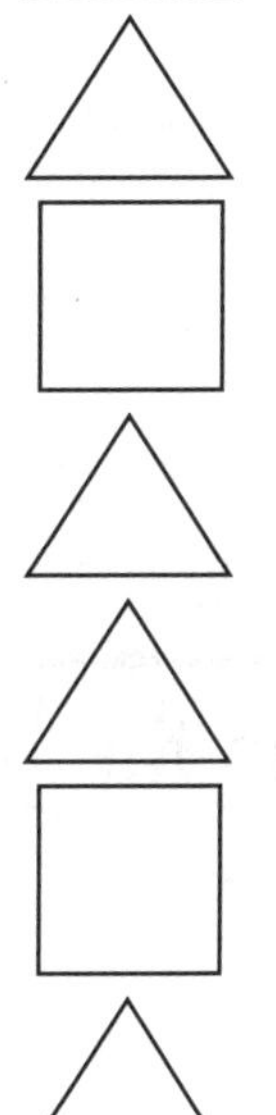
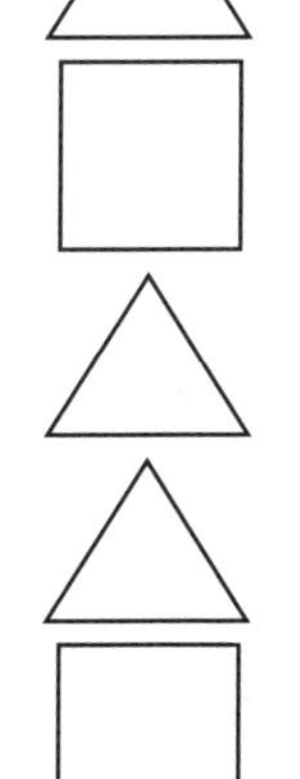
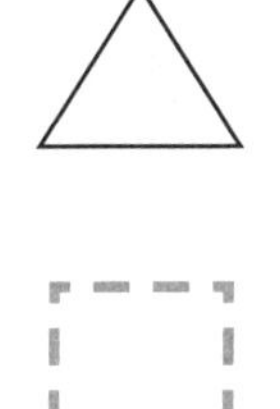

____

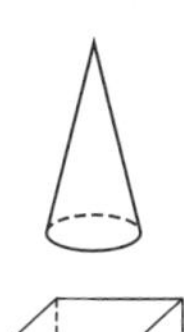
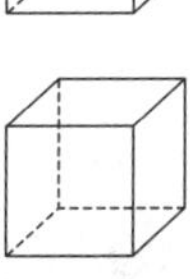

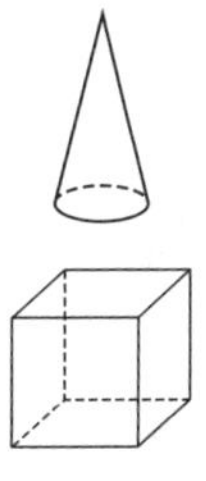

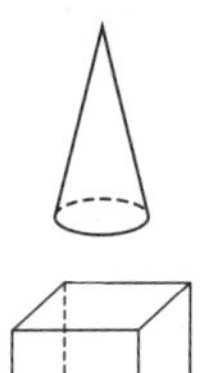

____

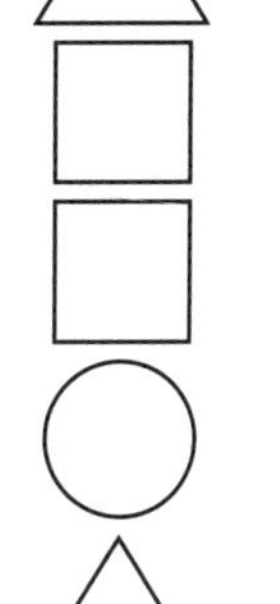

____

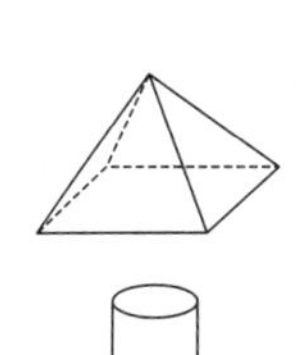
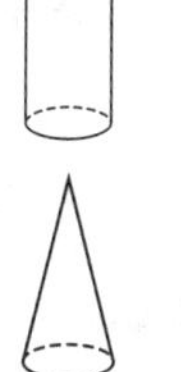
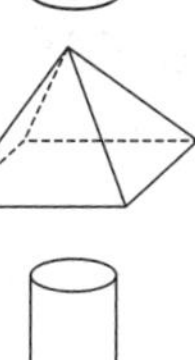
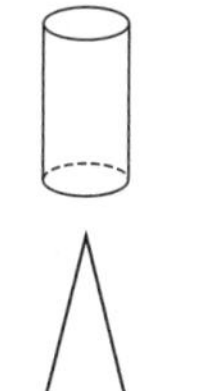
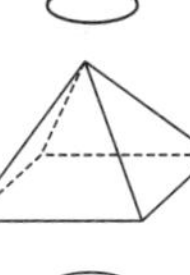
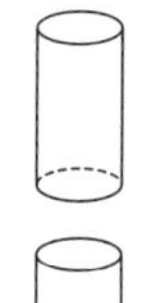

____

NAME ____________________

Lesson 9.5 Number Sentences

Make a related fact to solve. (Hint: Put the box after the equals sign.)

$9 - 4 = \square$ $\quad$ $17 - 9 = \square$ $\quad$ $8 + 5 = \square$ $\quad$ $14 - 6 = \square$

$\square = \underline{5}$ $\quad$ $\square = \underline{8}$ $\quad$ $\square = \underline{13}$ $\quad$ $\square = \underline{9}$

What number goes in the box?

$4 + \square = 9$ $\quad$ $\square + 9 = 17$ $\quad$ $\square - 5 = 8$ $\quad$ $14 - \square = 6$

Make a related fact to solve. Circle the number that goes in the box.

$\begin{array}{r} 16 \\ + \square \\ \hline 9 \end{array}$ $\quad$ $\begin{array}{r} 16 \\ - \ 9 \\ \hline (7) \end{array}$ $\quad$ $\begin{array}{r} 4 \\ + \square \\ \hline 7 \end{array}$ $\quad$ $\begin{array}{r} \square \\ + \ 6 \\ \hline 13 \end{array}$ $\quad$ $\begin{array}{r} \square \\ + \ 3 \\ \hline 11 \end{array}$

$\square + 4 = 11$ $\quad$ $8 - \square = 3$ $\quad$ $\square - 5 = 5$ $\quad$ $9 + \square = 15$

$\underline{11 - 4 = 7}$ $\quad$ ________ $\quad$ ________ $\quad$ ________

$\begin{array}{r} \square \\ + \ 1 \\ \hline 6 \end{array}$ $\quad$ $\begin{array}{r} 12 \\ - \square \\ \hline 7 \end{array}$ $\quad$ $\begin{array}{r} 5 \\ + \square \\ \hline 14 \end{array}$ $\quad$ $\begin{array}{r} \square \\ - \ 3 \\ \hline 9 \end{array}$

$14 - \square = 7$ $\quad$ $8 + \square = 10$ $\quad$ $\square + 8 = 15$ $\quad$ $\square - 3 = 6$

________ $\quad$ ________ $\quad$ ________ $\quad$ ________

NAME ______________________

Lesson 9.5 Problem Solving

Write the problems in numbers. Use a box to show the unknown number. Then, use a related fact to solve.

Luis has 3 fish. Tim has some fish, too. Together they have 8 fish.

How many fish does Tim have?

$3 + \square = 8$ $8 - 3 = \square$ $\square = 5$

Jason buys 15 items at the store.

He brings some to his grandmother. He now has 6 items.

How many items did he give to his grandmother?

______________ ______________ $\square$ = ______

Shannon and Keith made 17 cupcakes.

Shannon does not know how many cupcakes she made.

Keith knows he made 8. How many cupcakes did Shannon make?

______________ ______________ 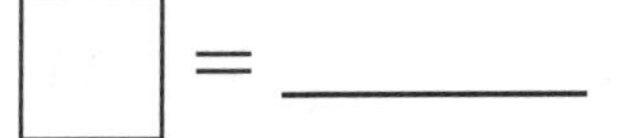

Alicia picked some flowers. She gave 6 to her mother.

She has 6 left. How many flowers did she pick?

 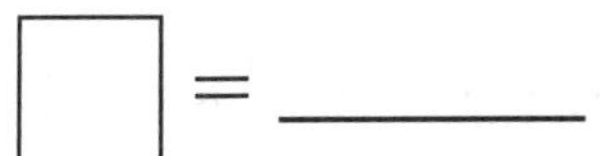

Julia had some computer games. She gave 4 to a friend.

She has 5 left. How many games did she start with?

______________ ______________ $\square$ = ______

NAME ____________________

Lesson 9.5 Problem Solving

Write the problems in numbers. Use a box to show the unknown number. Then, use a related fact to solve.

Mei has 16 stamps. She trades some of them.

She keeps 9. How many stamps does she trade?

16 − □ = 9　　16 − 9 = □　　□ = 7

Joe plants 4 trees. His mother also plants some trees.

Together they plant 12 trees. How many does his mother plant?

________　　________　　□ = ____

Tameka borrowed some books last week.

She borrowed 6 books this week. She borrowed 10 books in all.

How many books did she borrow last week?

________　　________　　□ = ____

Rafael plants 15 seeds. Some of them do not grow.

9 seeds grow into plants. How many do not grow?

________　　________　　□ = ____

Grace has some books about dance.

She buys 3 more. Now she has 7 books about dance.

How many did she have to begin with?

________　　________　　□ = ____

NAME ____________________

Check What You Learned

Preparing for Algebra

Use subtraction to find the number pattern.
Write the number that comes next.

1 2 5 10 17 26 ____
+____ +____ +____ +____ +____ +____

4 7 10 13 16 19 ____
+____ +____ +____ +____ +____ +____

Circle the object in the box that should be next in the pattern.

Draw the next shape in the pattern.

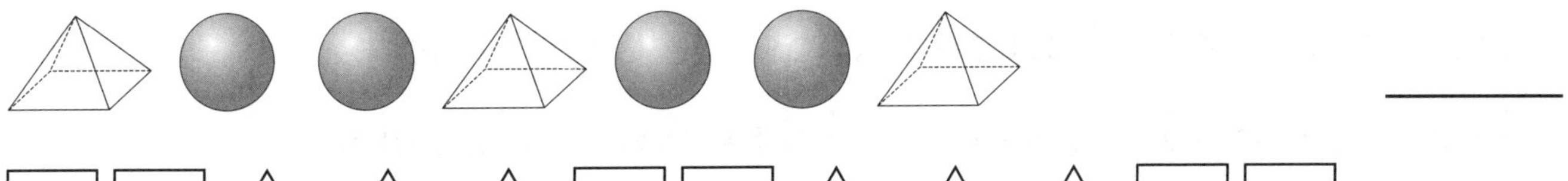

Draw the next 2 shapes in the pattern.

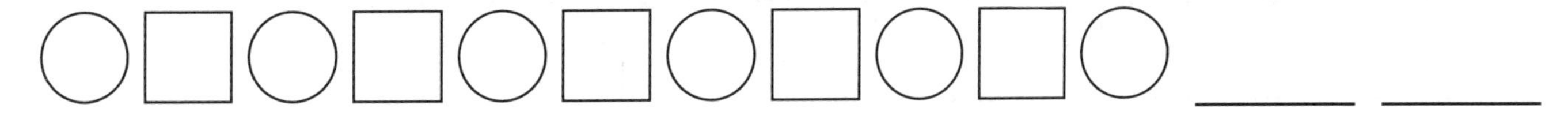

CHAPTER 9 POSTTEST

NAME ____________________

Check What You Learned

Preparing for Algebra

Make a related fact to solve. Circle the number that goes in the box.

$$15 - \square = 8 \qquad 8 + \square = 13 \qquad \square - 3 = 9 \qquad \square + 7 = 9$$

$\square + 4 = 11$ ______ $14 - \square = 7$ ______ $5 + \square = 8$ ______ $\square - 6 = 4$ ______

Write the number of each object in the pattern. Circle the object in the box that should be next.

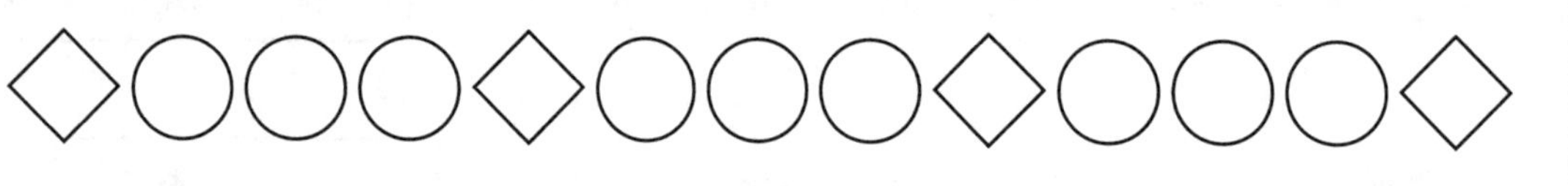

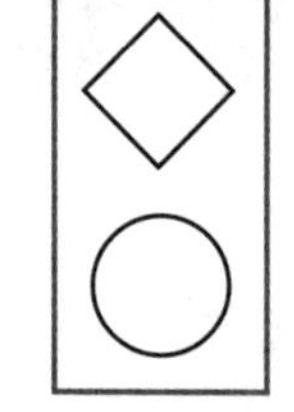

______

Write the problems in numbers. Use a box to show the unknown number. Then, use a related fact to solve.

Jordan has some baseball cards. He buys 5 more.
Now he has 12. How many did he have to begin with?

______ ______ 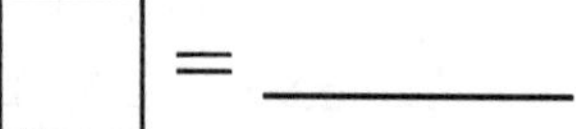

There are 15 flowers in the garden. Karen picks some.
Now there are 6. How many flowers did Karen pick?

______ ______ 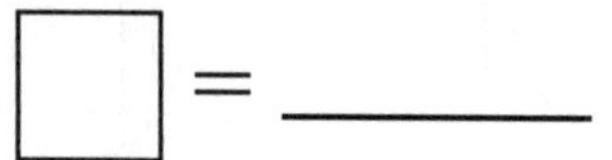

NAME ____________________

Final Test Chapters 1–9

Add.

$\begin{array}{r} 9 \\ +8 \\ \hline \end{array}$	$\begin{array}{r} 26 \\ +34 \\ \hline \end{array}$	$\begin{array}{r} 7 \\ +3 \\ \hline \end{array}$	$\begin{array}{r} 42 \\ +17 \\ \hline \end{array}$	$\begin{array}{r} 7 \\ +6 \\ \hline \end{array}$	$\begin{array}{r} 33 \\ +45 \\ \hline \end{array}$
$\begin{array}{r} 23 \\ +16 \\ \hline \end{array}$	$\begin{array}{r} 5 \\ +0 \\ \hline \end{array}$	$\begin{array}{r} 47 \\ +\ 9 \\ \hline \end{array}$	$\begin{array}{r} 74 \\ +17 \\ \hline \end{array}$	$\begin{array}{r} 8 \\ +7 \\ \hline \end{array}$	$\begin{array}{r} 16 \\ 20 \\ +32 \\ \hline \end{array}$

Subtract.

$\begin{array}{r} 79 \\ -36 \\ \hline \end{array}$	$\begin{array}{r} 15 \\ -\ 9 \\ \hline \end{array}$	$\begin{array}{r} 75 \\ -36 \\ \hline \end{array}$	$\begin{array}{r} 7 \\ -7 \\ \hline \end{array}$	$\begin{array}{r} 68 \\ -22 \\ \hline \end{array}$	$\begin{array}{r} 17 \\ -\ 8 \\ \hline \end{array}$
$\begin{array}{r} 11 \\ -\ 3 \\ \hline \end{array}$	$\begin{array}{r} 82 \\ -79 \\ \hline \end{array}$	$\begin{array}{r} 4 \\ -3 \\ \hline \end{array}$	$\begin{array}{r} 50 \\ -23 \\ \hline \end{array}$	$\begin{array}{r} 9 \\ -5 \\ \hline \end{array}$	$\begin{array}{r} 78 \\ -55 \\ \hline \end{array}$

Circle the object that should be next in the pattern.

Draw the next 2 objects in the pattern.

○ △ □ □ ○ △ □ □ ○ △ □ □ ○ ______ ______

Use a related fact to solve. Circle the number that goes in the box.

$4 + \square = 11$ $8 - \square = 7$ $\square + 3 = 12$ $\square - 5 = 9$

____________ ____________ ____________ ____________

NAME ___________________

Final Test Chapters 1–9

Count how many. Write the number word. Write odd or even.

_______________ __________

_______________ __________

Count tens and ones.

_____ tens _____ ones = _______¢

_____ tens _____ ones = _______¢

Write the number.

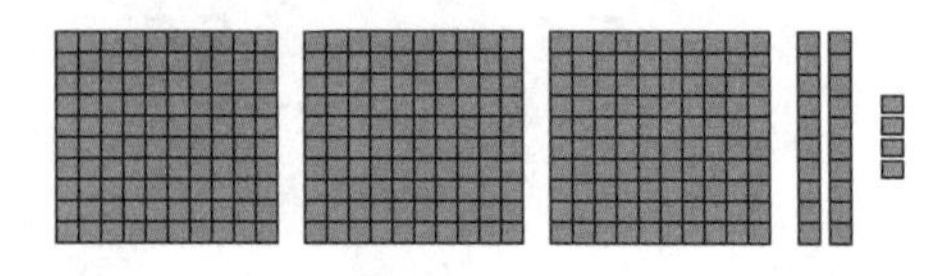

____

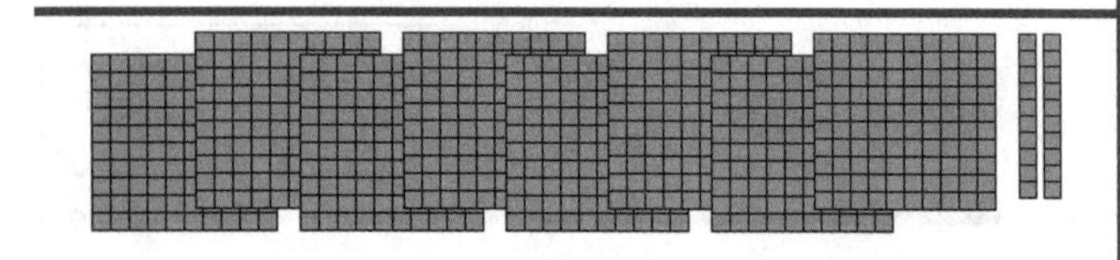

____

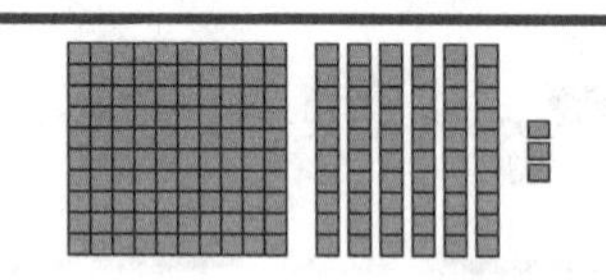

____

Write the fraction shown. Use numbers.

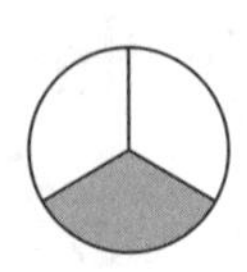

____

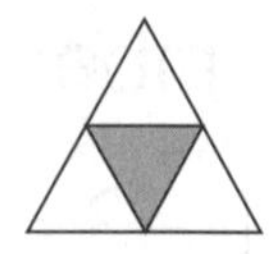

____

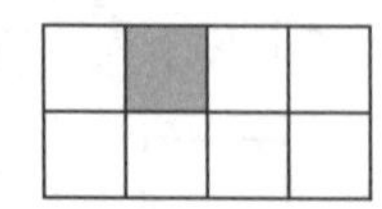

____

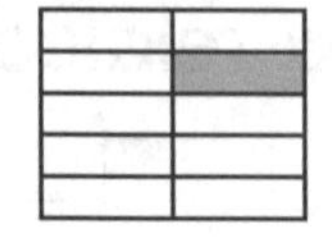

____

NAME ____________________

Final Test Chapters 1–9

Name the plane shape.

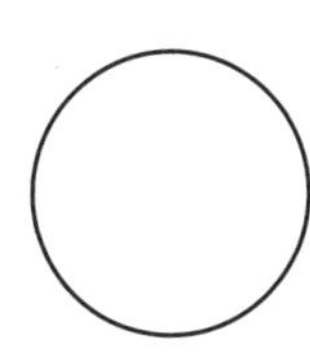

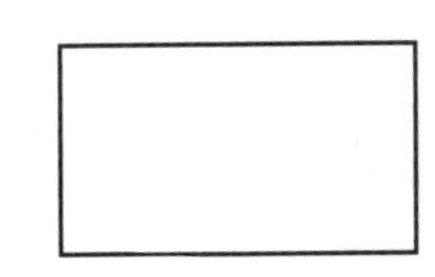

__________ __________

Draw a triangle.

Draw a cone.

Circle the named shape.

rectangular solid 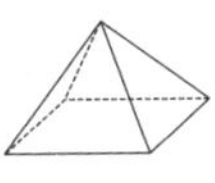 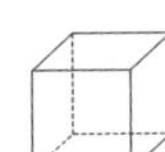 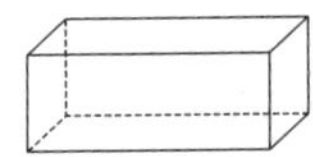

sphere   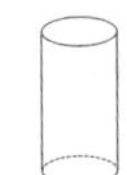

Use the calendar to answer the questions.

How many days are in the month? _____

How many Mondays are in the month? _____

What day is July 4th? __________

July						
S	M	T	W	Th	F	Sa
					1	2
3	4	5	6	7	8	9
10	11	12	13	14	15	16
17	18	19	20	21	22	23
24	25	26	37	28	29	30
31						

Measure. Use a centimeter ruler.

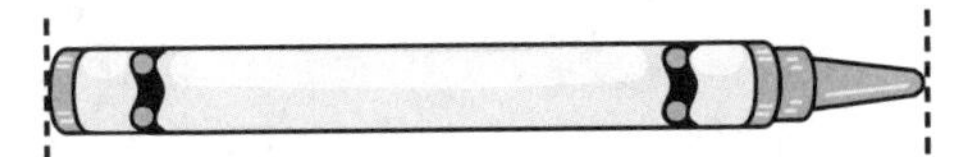

_____ centimeters

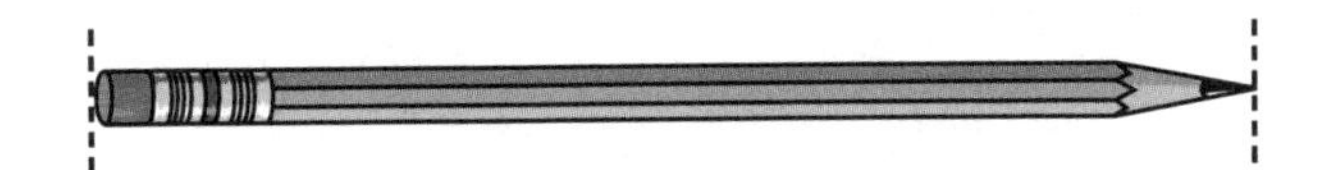

_____ centimeters

Write the time shown.

_____ : _____

_____ : _____

Write the °F and °C temperatures. Round °F to the nearest 10.

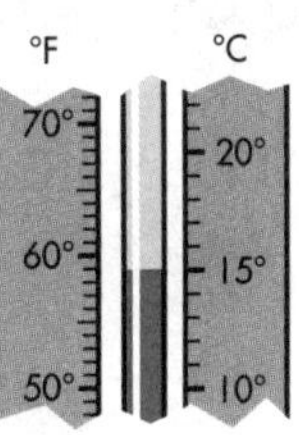

_____ °F

_____ °C

CHAPTERS 1–9 FINAL TEST

NAME ____________________

Final Test Chapters 1–9

Callie asked her classmates about their favorite drinks. She made this picture graph with the results.

= 2 students

Our Favorite Drinks

Milk	
Apple Juice	
Grape Juice	
Other	

Use the graph to answer these questions.

How many students does each glass represent? ________

How many students chose grape juice? ________

Which drink did most students choose? ________

Add the money amounts shown.

¢

\+ ¢

¢

SHOW YOUR WORK

Write numbers to solve the problem.

The second-grade class plants 23 .

The third-grade class plants 26  .

How many more does the third grade plant? ________

NAME ________________________________ DATE ____________

Scoring Record for Posttests, Mid-Test, and Final Test

		Performance			
Chapter Posttest	Your Score	Excellent	Very Good	Fair	Needs Improvement
1	____ of 34	33–34	28–32	21–27	20 or fewer
2	____ of 41	39–41	34–38	26–33	25 or fewer
3	____ of 41	39–41	34–38	26–33	25 or fewer
4	____ of 35	34–35	29–33	22–28	21 or fewer
5	____ of 75	71–75	61–70	46–60	45 or fewer
6	____ of 40	38–40	33–37	25–32	24 or fewer
7	____ of 16	16	14–15	11–13	10 or fewer
8	____ of 18	18	15–17	12–14	11 or fewer
9	____ of 35	34–35	29–33	22–28	21 or fewer
Mid-Test	____ of 77	73–77	63–72	47–62	46 or fewer
Final Test	____ of 69	65–69	56–64	42–55	41 or fewer

Record your test score in the Your Score column. See where your score falls in the Performance columns. Your score is based on the total number of required responses. If your score is fair or needs improvement, review the chapter material.

Grade 2 Answers

Chapter 1

Pretest, page 1

fifth; 2, 4, 24; 1, 6, 16
6, 3, 63; 4, 8, 48
even; odd

Pretest, page 2

13; thirteen
8; eight
20, 30, 50, 60
5, 7, 5, 2
10, 20, 25, 30

Lesson 1.1, page 3

4, 6, 3, 2
9, 8, 10
7, 0, 1, 5
seven, one
four, three
nine
two, six
eight
ten

Lesson 1.1, page 4

11, 12, 13, 14, 15
16, 17, 18, 19, 20
eighteen
twelve
sixteen
thirteen
twenty
19
11
15
14
17

Lesson 1.2, page 5

sixth
fifth

fourth
second, seventh
seventh
second

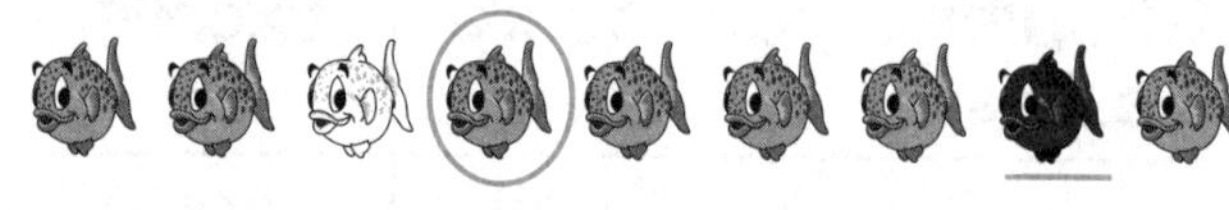

Lesson 1.2, page 6

eighth, seventeenth
sixth, tenth, twentieth

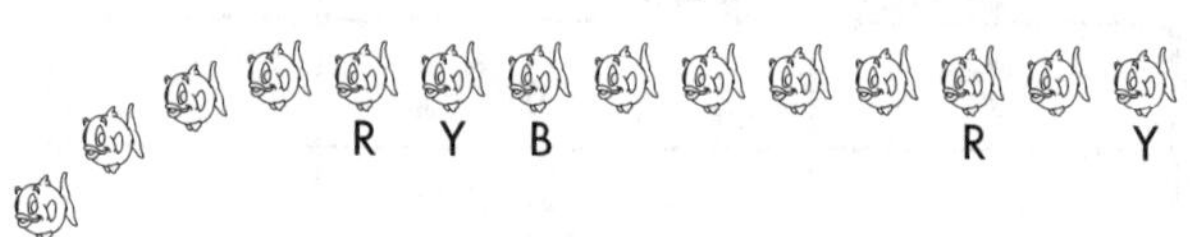

Y

B

Lesson 1.3, page 7

1, 2
3, 4
5, 6
7
8
9
10
1, 0, 1, 0

Grade 2 Answers

Lesson 1.4, page 8
1, 2, 12
1, 3, 13
1, 4, 14
1, 5, 15
1, 6, 16
1, 7, 17
1, 8, 18
1, 9, 19

Lesson 1.5, page 9
2, 1, 21; 2, 2, 22
2, 3, 23; 2, 4, 24
2, 5, 25; 2, 6, 26
2, 7, 27
2, 8, 28
2, 9, 29

Lesson 1.6, page 10
3, 0, 30; 3, 2, 32
3, 3, 33; 3, 6, 36
3, 8, 38; 4, 0, 40
4, 7, 47; 4, 9, 49

Lesson 1.7, page 11
5, 0, 50; 5, 1, 51
5, 3, 53; 6, 4, 64
6, 8, 68; 8, 5, 85
9, 0, 90; 9, 7, 97

Lesson 1.8, page 12
8, 14
15, 20, 30, 35
40, 50, 60
14, 16, 22
20, 30, 35, 55, 65, 75, 80
80, 60, 40, 30

Lesson 1.9, page 13
8, 10, 12
84, 88, 90
10, 20, 30

Lesson 1.9, page 14
55, 65, 75
20, 40, 50, 80, 90
80, 60, 40, 30, 20

Lesson 1.10, page 15
8, even; 5, odd

Lesson 1.10, page 16

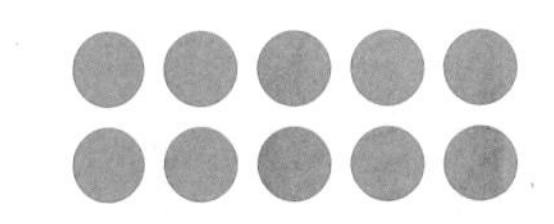

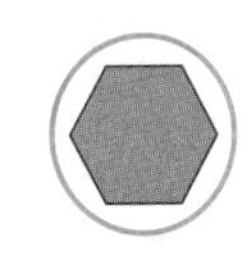

8, even; 3, odd
7, odd; 6, even

Lesson 1.11, page 17
6, 6, 6; 4, 4, 4
5, 3, 2; 6, 6, 6
1, 3, 4; 4, 3, 1
9, 3, 6; 6, 3, 9
1, 7, 8; 8, 7, 1

Lesson 1.12, page 18
4, 0; 3, 0
4, 2; 3, 0
2, 0; 2, 2

Posttest, page 19
22, 24, 28, 30
10, 15, 25, 30
7; seven
15; fifteen
4, 6, 46; 8, 4, 84

Posttest, page 20
0, 6, 6; 7, 3, 73
odd; even
3, 1
6, 9, 3, 9

Chapter 2

Pretest, page 21
16, 5, 2, 11, 7, 15
8, 10, 12, 4, 9, 17
3, 6, 13, 14, 12, 10
1, 7, 2, 5, 8, 9
7, 7, 3, 0, 8, 6
9, 3, 3, 7, 8, 5

Grade 2 Answers

Pretest, page 22

$$\begin{array}{r} 6 \\ +8 \\ \hline 14 \end{array}$$

$$\begin{array}{r} 17 \\ -\ 8 \\ \hline 9 \end{array}$$

$$\begin{array}{r} 15 \\ -\ 6 \\ \hline 9 \end{array}$$

$$\begin{array}{r} 8 \\ -\ 6 \\ \hline 2 \end{array}$$

$$\begin{array}{r} 8 \\ +\ 7 \\ \hline 15 \end{array}$$

Lesson 2.1, page 23
5, 4, 5, 4, 1, 3
2, 2, 5, 3, 4, 3
4, 0, 5, 4, 4, 2
1, 5, 3, 4, 5, 2
0, 2 ,5, 3, 4, 5

Lesson 2.2, page 24
3, 0, 0, 1, 3, 3
0, 1, 0, 1, 2, 4
4, 2, 2, 0, 2, 3
1, 5, 0, 3, 0, 0
1, 3, 1, 2, 3, 4

Lesson 2.3, page 25
6, 8, 7, 7, 8, 8
6, 6, 7, 6, 8, 8
7, 7, 8, 7, 6, 6
8, 8, 7, 8, 6, 7
8, 8, 7, 6, 6, 7

Lesson 2.4, page 26
4, 6, 3, 4, 3, 4
7, 1, 2, 0, 5, 0
5, 6, 3, 1, 2, 2
0, 6, 5, 7, 8, 1
4, 5, 4, 4, 0, 3

Lesson 2.5, page 27
9, 10, 10, 9, 10, 9
9, 9, 10, 10, 10, 9
9, 9, 9, 9, 9, 10
9, 10, 10, 10, 9, 9
9, 10, 10, 10, 10, 9

Lesson 2.6, page 28
3, 5, 6, 6, 1, 2
9, 1, 4, 2, 8, 4
9, 5, 3, 7, 7, 10
0, 8, 6, 1, 9, 4
1, 5, 8, 2, 2, 7

Lesson 2.7, page 29
12, 11, 13, 11, 12, 11
12, 13, 12, 12, 11, 13
11, 12, 11, 13, 11, 13
13, 11, 12, 12, 13, 11
11, 12, 12, 13, 13, 11

Lesson 2.8, page 30
8, 2, 4, 7, 9, 5
3, 7, 5, 9, 6, 6
9, 4, 3, 8, 6, 8
7, 8, 4, 6, 7, 4
9, 7, 3, 9, 5, 5

Lesson 2.9, page 31
14, 12, 16, 13, 14, 11
11, 14, 13, 16, 12, 16
14, 15, 12, 11, 14, 13
15, 12, 12, 11, 15, 15
13, 14, 11, 16, 11 ,14

Lesson 2.10, page 32
5, 7, 5, 8, 7, 4
5, 9, 6, 7, 9, 6
9, 7, 8, 2, 6, 8
4, 3, 6, 8, 9, 9
7, 7, 5, 8, 5, 7

Grade 2 Answers

Lesson 2.11, page 33

18, 17, 16, 13, 11, 12
14, 11, 15, 12, 15, 17
17, 14, 12, 13, 12, 14
11, 13, 18, 15 ,12 ,11
11, 14, 13, 17, 16, 11

Lesson 2.12, page 34

9, 8, 6, 8, 6, 4
3, 9, 8, 5, 7, 6
8, 6, 8, 3, 5, 9
8, 9, 5, 4, 6, 7
2, 9, 9, 4, 7, 8

Lesson 2.13, page 35

$$\begin{array}{r} 13 \\ -\ 7 \\ \hline 6 \end{array}$$

$$\begin{array}{r} 8 \\ +\ 6 \\ \hline 14 \end{array}$$

$$\begin{array}{r} 15 \\ -\ 7 \\ \hline 8 \end{array}$$

$$\begin{array}{r} 6 \\ +\ 3 \\ \hline 9 \end{array}$$

$$\begin{array}{r} 18 \\ -\ 9 \\ \hline 9 \end{array}$$

Lesson 2.13, page 36

subtract; $\begin{array}{r} 12 \\ -\ 6 \\ \hline 6 \end{array}$

subtract; $\begin{array}{r} 14 \\ -\ 5 \\ \hline 9 \end{array}$

add; $\begin{array}{r} 6 \\ +\ 7 \\ \hline 13 \end{array}$

add; $\begin{array}{r} 5 \\ +\ 4 \\ \hline 9 \end{array}$

Posttest, page 37

7, 10, 12, 3, 16, 18
9, 13, 6, 4, 14, 5
8, 9, 15, 17, 11, 12
9, 6, 2, 6, 1, 5
7, 9, 0, 9, 6, 6
8, 9, 4, 0, 3, 0

Posttest, page 38

$$\begin{array}{r} 15 \\ -\ 6 \\ \hline 9 \end{array}$$

$$\begin{array}{r} 7 \\ +\ 5 \\ \hline 12 \end{array}$$

$$\begin{array}{r} 12 \\ -\ 5 \\ \hline 7 \end{array}$$

$$\begin{array}{r} 9 \\ +\ 9 \\ \hline 18 \end{array}$$

$$\begin{array}{r} 11 \\ -\ 3 \\ \hline 8 \end{array}$$

Chapter 3

Pretest, page 39

57, 74, 98, 59, 69
59, 91, 39, 58, 93
39, 68, 78, 96, 59
5, 27, 20, 13, 22
24, 27, 50, 17, 3
35, 31, 6, 20, 22

Pretest, page 40

$$\begin{array}{r} 24 \\ +41 \\ \hline 65 \end{array}$$

$$\begin{array}{r} 36 \\ +22 \\ \hline 58 \end{array}$$

$$\begin{array}{r} 37 \\ -25 \\ \hline 12 \end{array}$$

$$\begin{array}{r} 58 \\ -45 \\ \hline 13 \end{array}$$

$$\begin{array}{r} 53¢ \\ -41¢ \\ \hline 12¢ \end{array}$$

Lesson 3.1, page 41

64, 79, 79, 87, 74
76, 48, 87, 94, 88
91, 89, 98, 69, 89
87, 69, 85, 79, 59
95, 77, 98, 59, 53

Lesson 3.1, page 42

69, 97, 39, 79, 75
99, 79, 39, 57, 86
56, 88, 49, 67, 68
49, 68, 63, 76, 89
56, 69, 56, 48, 99
94, 76, 78, 58, 77
78, 89, 78, 98, 63

Lesson 3.2, page 43

67, 89, 85, 79, 39
69, 84, 77, 47, 87
89, 57, 89, 96, 69
85, 27, 94, 89, 40
96, 77, 67, 84, 65
69, 94, 86, 67, 87
49, 39, 54, 87, 77

Lesson 3.2, page 44

$$\begin{array}{r} 10 \\ +11 \\ \hline 21 \end{array}$$

$$\begin{array}{r} 42 \\ +33 \\ \hline 75 \end{array}$$

$$\begin{array}{r} 13 \\ +20 \\ \hline 33 \end{array}$$

$$\begin{array}{r} 14 \\ +22 \\ \hline 36 \end{array}$$

$$\begin{array}{r} 32 \\ +27 \\ \hline 59 \end{array}$$

Lesson 3.3, page 45

10, 81, 12, 14, 52
16, 53, 30, 12, 15
21, 14, 33, 24, 26
11, 30, 60, 31, 22
5, 14, 10, 62, 5

Lesson 3.3, page 46

11, 23, 25, 50, 14
13, 26, 21, 33, 31
52, 24, 11, 35, 20
33, 42, 17, 10, 24
91, 14, 4, 31, 12
14, 90, 34, 32, 41
25, 61, 62, 13, 11

Lesson 3.4, page 47

22, 34, 10, 16, 6
72, 18, 3, 60, 45
25, 32, 43, 45, 1
35, 43, 54, 40, 21
15, 32, 51, 40, 13
80, 60, 14, 74, 21
43, 20, 26, 18, 22

Lesson 3.4, page 48

$$\begin{array}{r} 28 \\ -10 \\ \hline 18 \end{array}$$

$$\begin{array}{r} 32 \\ -30 \\ \hline 2 \end{array}$$

$$\begin{array}{r} 65 \\ -22 \\ \hline 43 \end{array}$$

$$\begin{array}{r} 59 \\ -44 \\ \hline 15 \end{array}$$

$$\begin{array}{r} 37 \\ -12 \\ \hline 25 \end{array}$$

Lesson 3.5, page 49

69, 88, 87, 68, 96
87, 49, 87, 65, 59
69, 56, 58, 47, 66
79, 39, 77, 68, 88

Grade 2 Answers

Lesson 3.5, page 50

$$\begin{array}{r} 10 \\ 12 \\ +25 \\ \hline 47 \end{array}$$

$$\begin{array}{r} 14 \\ 15 \\ +20 \\ \hline 49 \end{array}$$

$$\begin{array}{r} 6 \\ 22 \\ +30 \\ \hline 58 \end{array}$$

$$\begin{array}{r} 32 \\ 26 \\ +10 \\ \hline 68 \end{array}$$

$$\begin{array}{r} 14 \\ 23 \\ +30 \\ \hline 67 \end{array}$$

Lesson 3.6, page 51

30¢ 32¢ (42¢ circled) 24¢

$$\begin{array}{r} 30¢ \\ +42¢ \\ \hline 72¢ \end{array} \qquad \begin{array}{r} 32¢ \\ +24¢ \\ \hline 56¢ \end{array}$$

$$\begin{array}{r} 30¢ \\ +32¢ \\ \hline 62¢ \end{array} \qquad \begin{array}{r} 42¢ \\ +24¢ \\ \hline 66¢ \end{array}$$

$$\begin{array}{r} 30¢ \\ 42¢ \\ +24¢ \\ \hline 96¢ \end{array} \qquad \begin{array}{r} 32¢ \\ 24¢ \\ +30¢ \\ \hline 86¢ \end{array}$$

Lesson 3.6, page 52

melon
apple

$$\begin{array}{r} 85¢ \\ -33¢ \\ \hline 52¢ \end{array} \qquad \begin{array}{r} 33¢ \\ -20¢ \\ \hline 13¢ \end{array}$$

$$\begin{array}{r} 35¢ \\ -20¢ \\ \hline 15¢ \end{array} \qquad \begin{array}{r} 85¢ \\ -20¢ \\ \hline 65¢ \end{array}$$

$$\begin{array}{r} 85¢ \\ -35¢ \\ \hline 50¢ \end{array} \qquad \begin{array}{r} 35¢ \\ -33¢ \\ \hline 2¢ \end{array}$$

Posttest, page 53

79, 36, 93, 66, 57, 99
47, 28, 59, 58, 84, 35
59, 68, 27, 87, 49, 69
16, 24, 13, 41, 50, 22
53, 70, 3, 33, 34, 24
73, 10, 25, 30, 17, 44

Posttest, page 54

$$\begin{array}{r} 15 \\ +14 \\ \hline 29 \end{array}$$

$$\begin{array}{r} 27 \\ +31 \\ \hline 58 \end{array}$$

$$\begin{array}{r} 35 \\ -24 \\ \hline 11 \end{array}$$

$$\begin{array}{r} 65 \\ -45 \\ \hline 20 \end{array}$$

$$\begin{array}{r} 45¢ \\ +52¢ \\ \hline 97¢ \end{array}$$

Chapter 4

Pretest, page 55

82, 75, 63, 90, 83
73, 41, 57, 72, 95
91, 61, 84, 60, 44
28, 5, 18, 6, 38
17, 28, 48, 22, 58
24, 7, 49, 74, 27

Pretest, page 56

$$\begin{array}{r} 61 \\ -45 \\ \hline 16 \end{array}$$

$$\begin{array}{r} 38 \\ +35 \\ \hline 73 \end{array}$$

$$\begin{array}{r} 72 \\ -44 \\ \hline 28 \end{array}$$

$$\begin{array}{r} 45 \\ +46 \\ \hline 91 \end{array}$$

$$\begin{array}{r} 95 \\ -38 \\ \hline 57 \end{array}$$

Lesson 4.1, page 57

81, 92, 64, 37, 82
92, 96, 84, 81, 36
72, 62, 51, 92, 85
70, 73, 70, 30, 91

Lesson 4.1, page 58

90, 63, 70, 90, 64
50, 83, 60, 72, 42
71, 91, 80, 85, 60
55, 80, 41, 84, 70
70, 82, 61, 60, 82
73, 71, 64, 47, 81

Lesson 4.2, page 59

71, 51, 83, 60, 64
73, 61, 60, 75, 67
41, 82, 92, 52, 92
53, 51, 71, 40, 81
60, 82, 92, 65, 72
90, 83, 63, 84, 85

Lesson 4.2, page 60

$$\begin{array}{r} 35 \\ +39 \\ \hline 74 \end{array}$$

$$\begin{array}{r} 48 \\ +36 \\ \hline 84 \end{array}$$

$$\begin{array}{r} 33 \\ +28 \\ \hline 61 \end{array}$$

$$\begin{array}{r} 15 \\ +\ 9 \\ \hline 24 \end{array}$$

$$\begin{array}{r} 15 \\ +16 \\ \hline 31 \end{array}$$

Lesson 4.3, page 61

29, 12, 29, 37, 7
57, 12, 27, 9, 57
15, 37, 5, 21, 19
38, 15, 15, 28, 56

Lesson 4.3, page 62

3, 9, 18, 88, 45
13, 16, 17, 9, 36
4, 26, 29, 9, 48
16, 38, 24, 8, 16
19, 8, 37, 16, 27

Lesson 4.4, page 63

9, 17, 9, 17, 26
36, 45, 9, 28, 27
4, 28, 48, 47, 36
15, 29, 46, 26, 48
36, 37, 8, 24, 49
18, 24, 9, 35, 56

Lesson 4.4, page 64

$$\begin{array}{r} 33 \\ -28 \\ \hline 5 \end{array}$$

$$\begin{array}{r} 25 \\ -19 \\ \hline 6 \end{array}$$

$$\begin{array}{r} 31 \\ -\ 8 \\ \hline 23 \end{array}$$

$$\begin{array}{r} 26 \\ -\ 8 \\ \hline 18 \end{array}$$

$$\begin{array}{r} 42 \\ -27 \\ \hline 15 \end{array}$$

Posttest, page 65

60, 84, 92, 73, 42
63, 80, 53, 72, 63
53, 50, 83, 60, 24
39, 9, 35, 6, 26
18, 6, 29, 38, 8
38, 26, 47, 9, 15

Grade 2 Answers

Posttest, page 66

$$\begin{array}{r} 50 \\ -38 \\ \hline 12 \end{array}$$

$$\begin{array}{r} 57 \\ +39 \\ \hline 96 \end{array}$$

$$\begin{array}{r} 60 \\ -51 \\ \hline 9 \end{array}$$

$$\begin{array}{r} 42 \\ -18 \\ \hline 24 \end{array}$$

$$\begin{array}{r} 37 \\ +29 \\ \hline 66 \end{array}$$

Mid-Test

Page 67

13, 43, 49, 14, 94, 9
17, 78, 81, 5, 69, 8
39, 78, 4, 12, 52, 68
36, 5, 9, 28, 9, 53
11, 7, 7, 10, 3, 37
8, 0, 12, 37, 8, 5

Page 68

17, seventeen, odd; 8, eight, even
50, 55, 65
14, 16, 20 ,22
2, 5, 25; 6, 0, 60
1, 7, 17; 4, 2, 42

Page 69

ninth
7, 4, 3, 7

4; 2

$$\begin{array}{r} 14 \\ +13 \\ \hline 27 \end{array}$$

$$\begin{array}{r} 34 \\ -\ 9 \\ \hline 25 \end{array}$$

Page 70

$$\begin{array}{r} 12 \\ -\ 3 \\ \hline 9 \end{array}$$

$$\begin{array}{r} 24 \\ 22 \\ +21 \\ \hline 67 \end{array}$$

$$\begin{array}{r} 30¢ \\ +33¢ \\ \hline 63¢ \end{array}$$

$$\begin{array}{r} 14 \\ +18 \\ \hline 32 \end{array}$$

$$\begin{array}{r} 45 \\ -24 \\ \hline 21 \end{array}$$

Chapter 5

Pretest, page 71

234; 306
496, 170
841
143; 658
80; 40; 30; 60
50; 50; 40; 80
10; 90; 20; 60
90; 70; 70; 20

Grade 2 Answers

Pretest, page 72

370, 380, 410, 420
740, 750, 770, 780
170, 180, 200, 210, 230, 240
455, 460, 475, 485
895, 905, 910, 920, 925
665, 670, 680, 685, 690, 695
100, 300, 400, 600, 700
800, 700, 500, 400, 200, 100
460 < 540; 918 > 908; 103 < 120
575 < 590; 260 > 240; 347 > 298
701 < 707; 647 < 742; 818 = 818
157 > 120; 450 > 370; 963 < 993

Lesson 5.1, page 73

1, 3, 7
1, 0, 9
1, 2, 2
1, 4, 6
1, 1, 4
1, 3, 0
1, 4, 8
1, 0, 3
1, 2, 2
1, 1, 2
1, 1, 9

Lesson 5.2, page 74

165; 178
184; 158
170; 152
180; 161
156; 199

Lesson 5.3, page 75

235; 309
324; 217
390; 289
241; 307
372; 263

Lesson 5.4, page 76

542; 435
640; 514
494; 671
433; 508
669; 586

Lesson 5.5, page 77

722
956; 809
840
774; 963
917
825

Lesson 5.6, page 78

313, 315, 316
417, 419, 421
610, 615, 620, 635
785, 795, 810 ,815
210, 220, 240, 260
360, 380, 390, 410, 420
200, 400, 500, 700
700, 600, 400, 300

Lesson 5.7, page 79

20; 60; 80; 90
40; 40; 20; 20
80; 90; 70; 30
50; 70; 50; 10
90; 30; 80; 60
60; 20; 70; 90
40; 50; 40; 80
10; 30; 60; 90
70; 50; 30; 20

Lesson 5.8, page 80

831 < 843; 436 > 379; 902 < 911
567 > 564; 306 < 401; 535 = 535
219 > 198; 739 > 730; 630 < 820
127 > 119; 407 < 610; 923 < 925
354 < 453; 802 > 792; 236 < 401
504 = 504; 402 < 408; 123 > 118
367 < 562; 760 > 740; 654 < 736
981 > 901; 391 < 491; 835 > 830

Posttest, page 81

412, 413, 415, 416
110, 115, 125, 130
565, 575, 580, 590
455, 460, 470, 475, 485, 490
660, 680, 690, 710
920, 930, 950, 970
800, 810, 840, 850, 870
30; 80; 70; 40
50; 40; 90; 70
10; 50; 90; 20
60; 60; 30; 90
30; 90; 60; 60
50; 10; 70; 100

Grade 2 Answers

Posttest, page 82

550; 129
218; 163
915; 183
405; 130
$410 < 501$; $653 < 672$; $946 > 942$
$378 > 350$; $741 > 561$; $143 < 206$
$850 > 796$; $235 < 253$; $510 > 501$
$910 > 850$; $476 = 476$; $385 < 405$

Chapter 6

Pretest, page 83

4, 1, $\frac{1}{4}$; 8, 1, $\frac{1}{8}$
10, 1, $\frac{1}{10}$; 2, 1, $\frac{1}{2}$
3, 1, $\frac{1}{3}$; 8, 1, $\frac{1}{8}$
10, 1, $\frac{1}{10}$; 2, 1, $\frac{1}{2}$

Pretest, page 84

$\frac{1}{3}$, one-third; $\frac{1}{4}$, one-fourth
$\frac{1}{10}$, one-tenth; $\frac{1}{2}$, one-half
$\frac{1}{4}$, one-fourth; $\frac{1}{8}$, one-eighth
$\frac{1}{3}$, one-third; $\frac{1}{10}$, one-tenth

Lesson 6.1, page 85

2, 1, $\frac{1}{2}$; 2, 1, $\frac{1}{2}$
2, 1, $\frac{1}{2}$; 2, 1, $\frac{1}{2}$
one-half; one-half

Lesson 6.2, page 86

3, 1, $\frac{1}{3}$; 3, 1, $\frac{1}{3}$
3, 1, $\frac{1}{3}$; 3, 1, $\frac{1}{3}$
one-third; one-third

Lesson 6.3, page 87

4, 1, $\frac{1}{4}$; 4, 1, $\frac{1}{4}$
4, 1, $\frac{1}{4}$; 4, 1, $\frac{1}{4}$
one-fourth; one-fourth

Lesson 6.4, page 88

8, 1, $\frac{1}{8}$; 8, 1, $\frac{1}{8}$
8, 1, $\frac{1}{8}$; 8, 1, $\frac{1}{8}$
one-eighth; one-eighth

Lesson 6.5, page 89

10, 1, $\frac{1}{10}$; 10, 1, $\frac{1}{10}$
10, 1, $\frac{1}{10}$; 10, 1, $\frac{1}{10}$
one-tenth; one-tenth

Lesson 6.6, page 90

$\frac{1}{3}$, one-third; $\frac{1}{10}$, one-tenth
$\frac{1}{2}$, one-half; $\frac{1}{8}$, one-eighth
$\frac{1}{4}$, one-fourth; $\frac{1}{3}$, one-third

Posttest, page 91

4, 1, $\frac{1}{4}$; 10, 1, $\frac{1}{10}$
8, 1, $\frac{1}{8}$; 3, 1, $\frac{1}{3}$
2, 1, $\frac{1}{2}$; 3, 1, $\frac{1}{3}$
4, 1, $\frac{1}{4}$; 10, 1, $\frac{1}{10}$

Posttest, page 92

$\frac{1}{8}$, one-eighth; $\frac{1}{2}$, one-half
$\frac{1}{10}$, one-tenth; $\frac{1}{4}$, one-fourth
$\frac{1}{3}$, one-third; $\frac{1}{8}$, one-eighth
$\frac{1}{4}$, one-fourth; $\frac{1}{2}$, one-half

Chapter 7

Pretest, page 93

4; 2
10
2:30; 7; 4:45
30
4

Pretest, page 94

cookie dough
7
12

$$\begin{array}{r} 25¢ \\ +30¢ \\ \hline 55¢ \end{array} \qquad \begin{array}{r} 15¢ \\ +50¢ \\ \hline 65¢ \end{array}$$

60, 15; is equal to

Lesson 7.1, page 95

$$\begin{array}{r} 20¢ \\ +50¢ \\ \hline 70¢ \end{array} \qquad \begin{array}{r} 50¢ \\ +15¢ \\ \hline 65¢ \end{array}$$

$$\begin{array}{r} 50¢ \\ +20¢ \\ \hline 70¢ \end{array} \qquad \begin{array}{r} 25¢ \\ +50¢ \\ \hline 75¢ \end{array}$$

$$\begin{array}{r} 25¢ \\ 20¢ \\ +10¢ \\ \hline 55¢ \end{array} \qquad \begin{array}{r} 50¢ \\ 20¢ \\ +25¢ \\ \hline 95¢ \end{array}$$

Grade 2 Answers

Lesson 7.1, page 96
65¢ is less than 70¢
50¢ is less than 60¢
45¢ is equal to 45¢
75¢ is greater than 60¢
65¢ is greater than 55¢
40¢ is less than 50¢

Lesson 7.2, page 97
7, 7:00; 12, 12:00; 11, 11:00
10, 10:00; 6, 6:00; 5, 5:00
9, 9:00; 8, 8:00; 2, 2:00

Lesson 7.3, page 98
4, 4:30; 10, 10:30; 11, 11:30
2, 2:30; 1, 1:30; 6, 6:30
5, 5:30; 9, 9:30; 3, 3:30

Lesson 7.4, page 99
6:45; 5:15; 10:15
3:45; 11:15; 7:45

Lesson 7.4, page 100
3, 4; 6; 3:30
5, 6; 9; 5:45
8; 12; 8:00
10, 11; 3; 10:15
4; 12; 4:00

Lesson 7.5, page 101
Tuesday
31
4
5
Friday
14

Lesson 7.5, page 102
7
12
February
April, June, September, November
January
December

Lesson 7.6, page 103
5 in.
3 in.; 2 in.
6 in.
1 in.; 3 in.

Lesson 7.6, page 104
1 in.; 5 in.
2 in.; 4 in.
3, 1, 3, 1, 8 in.; 2, 2, 2, 6 in.
1, 1, 1, 1, 4 in.; 2, 1, 2, 1, 6 in.

Lesson 7.7, page 105
8 cm; 4 cm; 9 cm
7 cm
17 cm

Lesson 7.7, page 106
6 cm; 5 cm
2 cm; 9 cm
6, 2, 6, 2, 16 cm; 6, 1, 6, 1, 14 cm
4, 4, 4, 4, 16 cm; 3, 3, 3, 3, 3, 15 cm

Lesson 7.8, page 107
9; 10; 8
10; 9; 4
6; 12; 10

Lesson 7.9, page 108
is less than; is greater than
is equal to; is less than
is equal to; is greater than

Lesson 7.10, page 109
60°F, 15°C; 70°F, 20°C
50°F, 10°C; 80°F, 25°C

Lesson 7.11, page 110
14
4
cat
7
25

Lesson 7.11, page 111
10
7
oranges
7
1
21

Grade 2 Answers

Lesson 7.11, page 112

40
12
Trina
11
17
5

Posttest, page 113

7; 5
9
is less than; 80°F, 25°C
31
Tuesday

Posttest, page 114

soccer
baseball
11
12:30; 6; 9:15

50¢	30¢
+25¢	+50¢
75¢	80¢

Chapter 8

Pretest, page 115

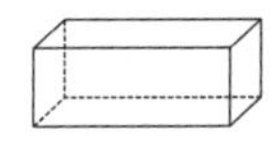

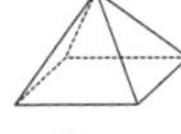

square; circle; triangle; rectangle

Pretest, page 116

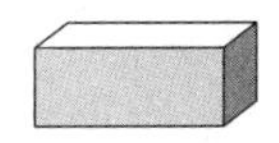 

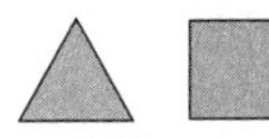

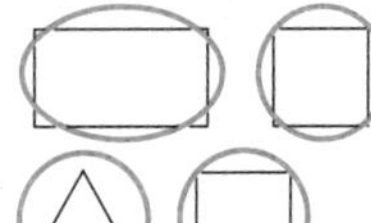

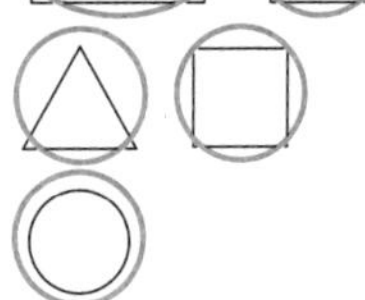

Lesson 8.1, page 117

circle; rectangle; triangle; circle
triangle; square; rectangle; square
rectangle; circle; square; triangle
square; triangle; rectangle; circle

Lesson 8.2, page 118

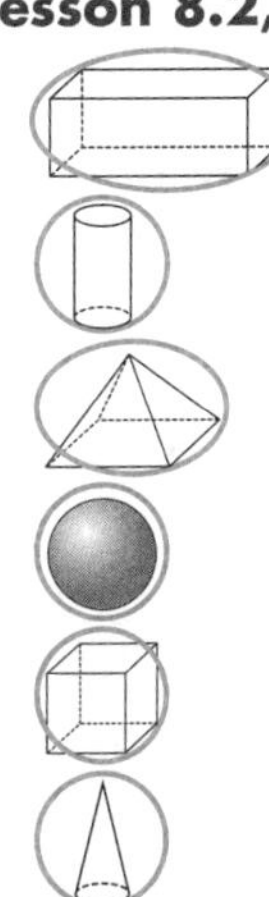

Lesson 8.3, page 119

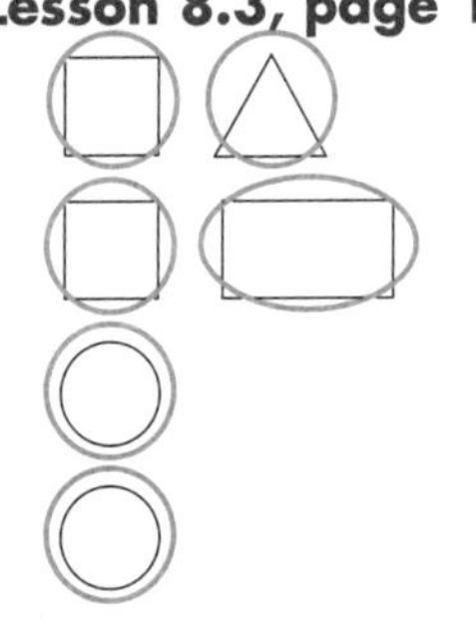

no
no
no

Lesson 8.4, page 120

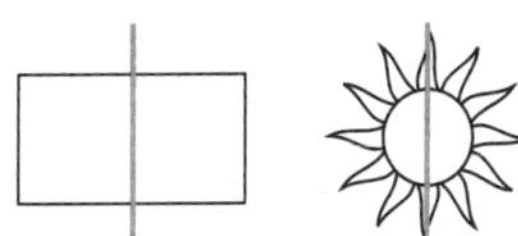  

Grade 2 Answers

Lesson 8.5, page 121

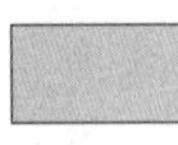

Lesson 8.5, page 122

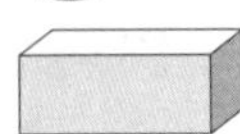
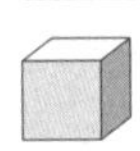
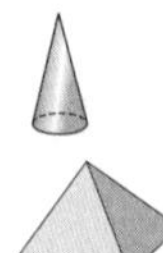

Posttest, page 123

triangle; square; rectangle; circle

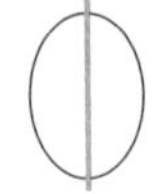  
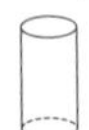
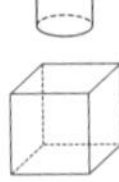

Posttest, page 124

 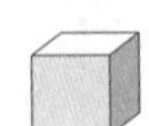

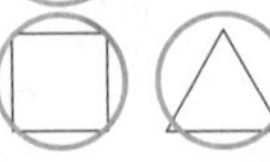

Chapter 9

Pretest, page 125

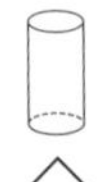

4, 4, 4, 4, 4, 21
2, 4, 6, 8, 10, 31

$11 - 2 = (9)$; $6 - 4 = (2)$; $8 + 4 = (12)$; $15 - 6 = (9)$

10	9	11	14
− 7	+ 9	− 6	− 8
(3)	(18)	(5)	(6)

Pretest, page 126

$9 + \square = 13$, $13 - 9 = \square$, $\square = 4$

$17 - \square = 9$, $17 - 9 = \square$, $\square = 8$

2, 1, 2, 1,

Lesson 9.1, page 127

Grade 2 Answers

Lesson 9.2, page 128

1, 3, 1, 3 

2, 2, 2, 2, 

1, 2, 1, 1, 2, 1, 

3, 2, 3, 

2, 1, 1, 2, 1, 1, 

Lesson 9.3, page 129

3, 3, 3, 3, 3, 3, 20
2, 4, 6, 8, 10, 12, 42
5, 5, 5, 5, 5, 5, 33
1, 3, 5, 7, 9, 11, 37

Lesson 9.4, page 130

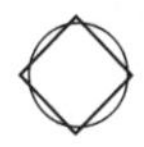

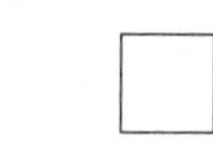

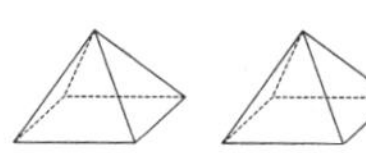

Lesson 9.4, page 131

 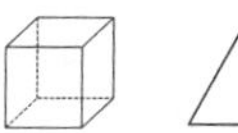 △ 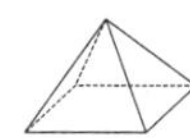

Lesson 9.5, page 132

5; 8; 13; 8

$16 - 9 = 7$ $7 - 4 = 3$ $13 - 6 = 7$ $11 - 3 = 8$

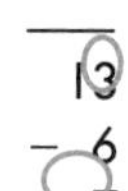

$11 - 4 = 7$; $8 - 3 = 5$; $5 + 5 = 10$; $15 - 9 = 6$

$6 - 1 = 5$ $12 - 7 = 5$ $14 - 5 = 9$ $9 + 3 = 12$

$14 - 7 = 7$; $10 - 8 = 2$; $15 - 8 = 7$; $6 + 3 = 9$

Lesson 9.5, page 133

$3 + \square = 8$, $8 - 3 = \square$, $\square = 5$

$15 - \square = 6$, $15 - 6 = \square$, $\square = 9$

$\square + 8 = 17$, $17 - 8 = \square$, $\square = 9$

$\square - 6 = 6$, $6 + 6 = \square$, $\square = 12$

$\square - 4 = 5$, $5 + 4 = \square$, $\square = 9$

Lesson 9.5, page 134

$16 - \square = 9$, $16 - 9 = \square$, $\square = 7$

$4 + \square = 12$, $12 - 4 = \square$, $\square = 8$

$\square + 6 = 10$, $10 - 6 = \square$, $\square = 4$

$15 - \square = 9$, $15 - 9 = \square$, $\square = 6$

$\square + 3 = 7$, $7 - 3 = \square$, $\square = 4$

Posttest, page 135

1, 3, 5, 7, 9, 11, 37
3, 3, 3, 3, 3, 3, 22

Grade 2 Answers

Posttest, page 136

$\begin{array}{r} 15 \\ -\ 8 \\ \hline 7 \end{array}$ $\begin{array}{r} 13 \\ -\ 8 \\ \hline 5 \end{array}$ $\begin{array}{r} 9 \\ +\ 3 \\ \hline 12 \end{array}$ $\begin{array}{r} 9 \\ -7 \\ \hline 2 \end{array}$

$11 - 4 = 7$; $14 - 7 = 7$; $8 - 5 = 3$; $4 + 6 = 10$

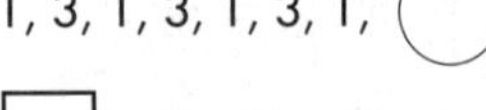

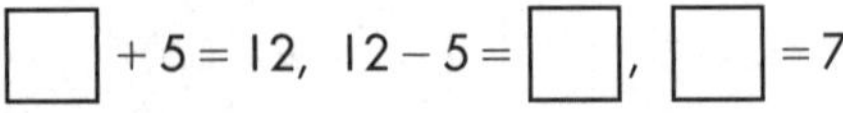

15 − ☐ = 6, 15 − 6 = ☐, ☐ = 9

Final Test

Page 137

17; 60; 10; 59; 13; 78
39; 5; 56; 91; 15; 68
43; 6; 39; 0; 46; 9
8; 3; 1; 27; 4; 23

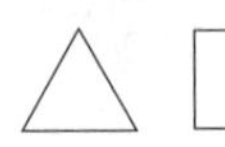

$11 - 4 = 7$; $8 - 7 = 1$; $12 - 3 = 9$; $5 + 9 = 14$

Page 138

fourteen, even; nine, odd
2, 7, 27; 6, 2, 62
324; 675
820; 163
$\frac{1}{3}$; $\frac{1}{4}$; $\frac{1}{8}$; $\frac{1}{10}$

Page 139

circle; rectangle;

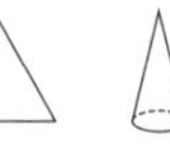

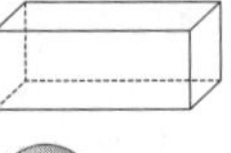

31
4
Monday
6; 8
9:15; 2:30; 60, 15

Page 140

2
6
milk

$\begin{array}{r} 50¢ \\ +30¢ \\ \hline 80¢ \end{array}$

$\begin{array}{r} 26 \\ -23 \\ \hline 3 \end{array}$